A Concrete Look at Nature

By the same author:

Our Own Baedeker: From "The New Yorker"
(with Russell Maloney)
Spider, Egg, and Microcosm
In Every War But One

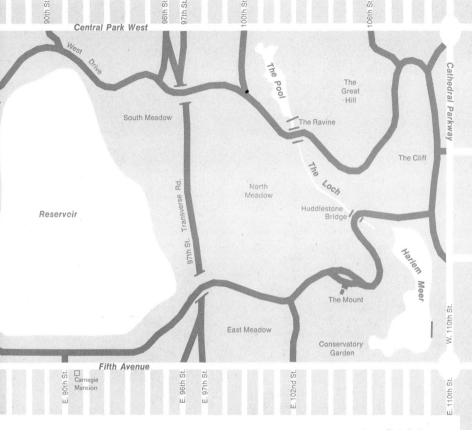

Map by Ed. Kenney

A Concrete Look at Nature
Central Park (and Other) Glimpses

By
Eugene Kinkead

Quadrangle/The New York Times Book Co.

Endpaper map by Edward Kenney, *The Conservationist*,
New York State Department of Environmental Conservation

Of the articles in this book, the following appeared
originally in *The New Yorker*: "Bird Walk," "Champion
Tree," "Big Rain," "State Bird," and "Bioluminescence."
They appear here in slightly different form.

Quadrangle/The New York Times Book Co.,
10 East 53 Street, New York, New York 10022.
Manufactured in the United States of America.
Published simultaneously in Canada by
Fitzhenry & Whiteside, Ltd., Toronto.

Drawings by Hope Sawyer Buyukmihci

Library of Congress Cataloging in Publication Data

Kinkhead, Eugene, 1906-
    A concrete look at nature.

    1. Natural history—New York (City)—Central
Park. 2. New York (City)—Parks—Central Park.
3. Natural history. I. Title.
QH105.N7K55 1974   574.9'747'1   74-77936
ISBN 0-8129-0471-0

To Katherine, with love

Contents

Preface

Since each section of this book at least begins at Central Park, a descriptive word or two about the place may be helpful to the reader. A masterpiece of outdoor planning through the genius of its designers, Frederick Law Olmsted and Calvert Vaux, the Park is unquestionably the most famous in the country, and one of the most celebrated in the world. Its 840 acres, constituting more than a square mile, lie approximately in the center of Manhattan, occupying better than 5 percent of the island, the Park area consisting of roughly 690 acres of land and 150 of water, of which the latter's largest body by far is the 106-acre city reservoir, the other principal bodies being the Lake, in the middle of the Park, the Harlem Meer, the Pond, the Belvedere Lake, the Pool, the Conservatory Water, and the Loch. One hundred thirty-seven and a half feet is the height of the Park's high point, Summit Rock, a spiny outcrop near the middle of the western edge, and the low point, 132 feet below this, is found on the shore of Harlem Meer in the northeast corner. A map of Central Park on the endpapers shows many of these landmarks and other features mentioned in the book.

Central Park is also the most frequented park in the nation. I was born near its northwest perimeter and, on my regular trips these days into the city, I continue to be one of the more than 12 million persons who visit it each year. For the general public it offers a variety of activities. Family pursuits include baby airing, carousel riding, supervised exercise for children in the peripheral playgrounds, dog walking, outdoor dining, pony rides, simple strolling, and zoo attendance. For the more or less athletic, there is bicycling, croquet, field hockey, football, lawn bowling, handball, hard and soft baseball, horseback riding, horseshoe pitching, paddle tennis, roller skating, shuffleboard, skiing, sledding, soccer, and tennis. Water sports comprise fishing, ice skating, rowboating, sailing model yachts, swimming, and wading. Concerts, dramatic plays, and storytelling for children are cultural events given in the Park. And chess and checker tables are there for games-minded adults—a diverse playground for a diverse city.

That special part of the public, too, the nature lover (toward whom this book is especially directed), can also find much to reward it there, particularly in the fields of botany and birds. Fighting against overuse and undermaintenance, the tulip trees and black locusts still bloom in May, the Virginia rose and red mulberry in June. In remote northern parts of the Park I have, in early spring, found even a native American wildflower, the dogtooth violet, still doggedly hanging on. The projected big-scale rehabilitation of the Park now being planned will, if it finally materializes, do much to help the flora, presently suffering greatly from erosion, vandalism, and lack of sufficient horticultural care.

Birds, the other great magnet for naturalists, use the Park as a migratory stop, and also nest and live there. Since it lies directly under the Atlantic Flyway, one of the four great migratory routes running north and south above our continent, and since its verdant space must appear as a welcome haven in the midst of a concrete desert to a bird overhead, it is small wonder that many weary fliers pitch downward to its branches for a respite, brief or lengthy, during their travels. In the four-score years or so that birders have been keeping records, a total of more than 250 species have been seen in the Park, more than a third of all the species known to appear on our continent north of Mexico. Furthermore, each year twelve to twenty species nest there as well, the number depending on the rise and fall of cover. Although it seems hard to believe today, such shy forms as the wood duck and bobwhite once made their homes there, too.

Moreover, the Park's resident wild mammals may seem surprising. Gone, alas, are such interesting habitants as the eastern flying squirrel and the muskrat, but there is the ubiquitous and saucy eastern gray squirrel and, astonishing as it may seem, the cottontail rabbit, which still somehow manages to survive amid the cyclists and the unleashed apartment-house dogs roaming the sward, not to mention all four species of New York's migratory bats—the big brown, hoary, red, and silver-haired—which currently spend time in the Park. Besides these, the sometimes unwholesome waters hold apparently healthy bullheads, goldfish, punkinseed sunfish, and yellow perch, as well as cray-fish, bullfrogs, water snails, roundworms, protozoa, and everywhere in the water and soil a host of microscopic life whose presence and importance is detailed at length in the book's two final chapters. Life in the Park, in other words, is durable and obstinate, refusing to be crowded out even in so inhospitable a setting as the middle of man-made Manhattan.

Now, a word or two of thanks to those who made this volume possible. Obviously, I am indebted to all the people whose names appear in the text. But a number of others must be mentioned as well: Miss Ann Breen, the public relations officer of the American Museum of Natural History; Henry L. Diamond, the former Commissioner of the New York State Department of Environmental Conservation; Miss Jean Goodwin, the former librarian of the National Audubon Society; S. Dillion Ripley, the Secretary of the Smithsonian Institution; and Mrs. Sonia Wedge, a librarian at the New York Botanical Garden.

Finally, my gratitude goes to William Shawn, the editor of *The New Yorker* magazine. He has consistently supported and encouraged these forays of mine into nature in the city, and elsewhere.

Eugene Kinkead
Colebrook, Connecticut

A Concrete Look at Nature

1
Bird Walk

Towering hundreds of feet in the air above Central Park is a periodically busy highroad that is missing from most maps of the region. It is the Atlantic Flyway, one of the four main routes running north and south on our continent over which migratory birds, as they have for bygone eons, pass each spring from the tropics to their nesting sites in higher latitudes and over which they return to warmer climes as the biting frost comes on. From its lofty reaches, as night fades in the cool spring-time sky, thousands of birds tumble gratefully downward to the young green of the Park, there to pause for

1

a few hours or longer before resuming their northward trip. In the branches of the trees and on the turf they rest and feed and, in the process, are often observed by local members of that growing coterie, the fellowship of bird-watchers.

Toward the middle of May in 1969, at the very height of the migrating season, I went for a bird walk in the Park with Mr. G. Stuart Keith. My companion was no ordinary bird-watcher. He was, instead, a British subject who, surprising as it may seem, held the North American record for the greatest number of species of birds seen by an individual during a calendar year. In 1956, following his graduation from Oxford, he spotted more than three-quarters of the 700-odd avian species known to appear on our continent north of Mexico. We met, by previous agreement, shortly before nine o'clock in the morning on Central Park West in front of the American Museum of Natural History, where Keith works as a dollar-a-year research associate in the Bird Department. The grand champion, a tall, good-looking, broad-shouldered man in his middle thirties, was hatless, and wore slacks, an odd jacket, and a blue tie with figures of green pelicans, over which a pair of binoculars hung on a leather strap around his neck. We entered the Park through the opening at Seventy-seventh Street, which is called Naturalists Gate and bears a plaque dedicating it to the thousands who study nature in the Park each year under the auspices of the Museum. Keith, a former junior officer in the King's Own Scottish Borderers, walked lightly and erect, while I shuffled after him with a pencil and small pad to list what we saw.

Just inside the entrance, I spotted a black bird somewhat larger than a robin sitting in an elm tree overlooking West Drive, the automobile road that meanders down the west side of the Park. "Boat-tailed grackle," I suggested.

Keith set me straight. "Purple grackle there," he said. "Boattails live in the South." He went on to say that lately the grackles had lost a species. The bronzed grackle, for years called a third member of the group, had recently been demoted to a subspecies of the purple. This was the work, Keith explained, of "the lumpers," an ornithological faction then in ascendancy over their opposite numbers, "the splitters." Thanks to the lumpers, the known total of bird species in the world has shrunk of late by a score or two to something around 8,800 species. A small but surprising number of these can be seen in Central Park, especially during migration, because of the Park's position under the Atlantic Flyway, which roughly follows our eastern coastline.

We continued toward the Lake, the largest body of purely scenic water in the Park, covering nearly twenty-two acres, and then started across it by way of Bank Rock Bridge, a wooden footway with ornamental iron balustrades. Leaning against the southerly balustrade, we paused to look for water birds. The Park was unbelievably quiet. Twelve million people walk through it each year, making it the most heavily used park of its size (a square mile or so) in the world, and the area around the Lake is the most heavily used. But we seemed to be the only people there at the time. A soft blue mist hung in the air. At that particular moment, it seemed, Keith and I could have been standing in a quiet corner of Arcady.

The mood changed quickly, as moods often do in New York. An immature ring-billed gull splashed into the water in front of us, off Hernshead Promontory, ducked his beak repeatedly into the water, flirted it over his back and sides with delighted wriggles, and drank long, satisfied gulps.

Behind us, to the north, was Bank Rock Bay, which was once a navigable part of the Lake but is now a shallow, muddy inlet where rowboats can no longer enter. A step or two after we had straightened up to resume our journey across the bridge, Keith showed me, halfway up a tall sweet-gum tree beyond the bay, a male Baltimore oriole. It was a startling sight against the new green in its wildly brilliant orange-and-black plumage. As we looked, it gave a series of rich, flutelike pipings. Suddenly it disappeared, and I complained of this to Keith. "Its bright colors break the pattern of its form," he said. "It's there, but hard to find—effective camouflage." The sweet whistle came again.

Among serious birders, hearing is practically as good as seeing—a fortunate circumstance, considering the number of birds that are either nocturnal or stubbornly shy about showing themselves during the day. Keith, as I was shortly to discover, has an excellent pair of ears. Ordinarily, he accepts his own aural identification of all birds except those he puts on his life list, a catalogue of all the species he has ever identified in the field. His worldwide life list is constantly being augmented by museum trips to remote regions which are usually productive in that regard. Even for experts, however, there are perils in the aural-identification method. Not long before our walk, Keith had heard what he could have sworn was a killdeer on the Museum's north lawn, in just the sort of spot where this long-legged, ploverlike bird of fields and pastures might pause for a breather during migration. Sight, however, proved it to be a starling, doing a superb impersonation, for which the only possible reward seemed to be the deliberate humiliation of the North American grand champion.

Just ahead of us, at the farther end of the bridge, rose the principal objective of our walk, the Ramble. Essentially a knoll of about thirty acres, the Ramble contains some of the highest land in the Park (the actual high point, a bit farther to the north, is Summit Rock, 137½ feet above sea level) and is the Park's most heavily planted area. It shelters a maze of macadam walks that wander past and over such natural and man-made features as Warbler Rock, the Summerhouse, Rustic Bridge, Azalea Pond, and the Swamp—the last two of which drain into the Gill, a threadlike stream that winds across the top of the Ramble and down its west side into the Lake. Around these features cluster some of the Park's oldest and largest trees, a few of the native oaks and locusts having stood there for years before the city took title to the land, in 1856. As elsewhere in the Park, much alien flora has been introduced. Korean mountain ash, English holly, and the Chinese pagoda tree, among other well-established immigrants, were before us and in early leaf. Here and there throughout the area, signs affixed to lampposts read, "The Ramble. A Natural Wild Life Preserve." The signs do not exaggerate. Some years back, the chairman of the Museum's Bird Department wrote in a letter to *The Times* that "there is probably no equal area of open countryside that can match the urban-bounded Ramble with respect to the concentration of birds that funnels down from the sky just before daybreaks of spring."

Partway up the slope of the Rample, Keith cocked his head. "Our first warbler," he said. "A parula." I couldn't hear it right off. But after straining a few moments I picked up a strident sound such as might be

produced by a very excited bumblebee—a steady *zee,*
zee, zee. Warblers in general, despite their name, are
rather poor singers. But, like many other poorly endowed creatures, they ignore the deficiency, and go
right on belting out their songs almost constantly
throughout the springtime. The parula, one of the smallest warblers (slightly more than half the size of a sparrow), is an undersized member of an undersized tribe
of sharp-billed insectivorous birds with rounded tails,
and it weighs scarcely more than a few king-size ciga-
rettes. In the United States, warblers number more than
fifty species, and during spring migration they are
among the bird-watcher's special joys—their gay colors
flitting through the fresh green like vagrant snippets of
rainbow. (On fall migration, they are in a state of sartorial degradation, wearing such generally washed-out,
nondescript shades that for most people the species are
impossible to tell apart.) The little parula—blue-backed
and yellow-breasted—was way up in an ancient pin-oak
tree whose small flowers, usually unnoticed by strollers
below, had drawn swarms of insects, which the parula,
between *zees,* was eating.

Aided by its superb vision, the parula was stuffing
itself. Whether active by day or night, a bird sees better
than other forms of life, thanks to a more highly developed eye, which is constructed much like that of other
vertebrates but has an especially large concentration of
rods and cones. These are the sensory cells of the retina
—the screen on which an optical image is translated into
nerve impulses and then transmitted to the brain over
the optic nerve. Cones provide color vision, while rods
provide definition and sensitivity to low levels of illumination. Although some specialized birds, like owls,
have only rods, for maximum night vision, most birds,
like warblers, have both. Rods and cones have a direct

blood supply, as does most tissue in vertebrates. But in birds a fleshy, comblike organ containing an abundant blood supply, the pecten, projects into the eye cavity from a point near the optic nerve. The pecten—restricted to birds and reptiles but more highly developed in birds —discharges food and oxygen, which diffuse through the viscous fluid in the eyeball, thus increasing the supply of nutrition available to the cells of the retina and making vision far and away a bird's primary sense. Gobble, *zee,* gobble, *zee* went the parula.

A migrating parula can take in enough food to expand its stomach to twice, and sometimes thrice, the normal size. And most of what it takes in is insects, which begin to reproduce in a prodigal fashion when the rays of the sun, falling more directly on the northern half of the world as a result of the seasonal tipping of the earth's axis, heat up the atmosphere and bring the warm weather to our hemisphere. Insects form by far the largest class of living things in the animal kingdom (over three-quarters of the 1 million or so species now known). Their breeding potential is enormous. One pair of houseflies, surviving and reproducing normally, could through their progeny within six months cover the earth forty-seven feet deep with houseflies. Fortunately, the diet of most migrant birds, whatever it might be at other times, greatly increases in protein as the breeding season approaches. They eat insects, and later on they cram insects into their nestlings.

Parulas winter in Mexico and the West Indies, and on an evening some three weeks earlier the one before us might have leaped into the air with others of its kind shortly after the sun sank in Yucatán. Probably to diminish predation, warblers and many small songbirds migrate by night, while such fast fliers as chimney swifts and larger, more boisterous types such as jays tend to be day migrants. Our parula and his companions, climbing gradually to a height of several thousand feet, would have barrelled out over the Gulf of Mexico, bound for Florida, some 400 miles away. Assuming a normal passage, the parula reached its objective sometime the next day, having maintained a cruising speed of from twenty to forty miles an hour, depending on the speed and direction of the wind. In Florida, the birds probably put down and rested for several days, restoring their depleted fat deposits for the largely overland trip up the Atlantic Flyway. (Fat is what a bird migrates on, since, per unit of weight, fat produces nearly twice as much energy as either protein or carbohydrate does, and in long-distance migrants fat deposits have to be large because a bird's bodily engine runs hot. Almost all bird temperatures exceed the temperature of human beings, many by more than fifteen degrees Fahrenheit.) Studies of small banded songbirds show that the Atlantic Flyway is usually taken in 200-mile jumps lasting from five to ten hours. The speed and altitude of migrants have been checked by radar, and small birds the size of the parula like to move along a half a mile or so up in the air. A parula flies as easily up there as lower down, partly because its main bones, like those of other birds, are hollow. Some of its bones contain air sacs, which are connected by other air sacs to the lungs. This arrangement not only cuts down on weight but also enables a bird to move maximum amounts of air through its lungs when it inhales and also when it exhales. Moreover, the dead-air space of the bird's respiratory system lies in the air sacs rather than in the lungs, as it does in mammals, permitting the bird's entire lung to be utilized in oxygen exchange. As a result, birds are able to extract much more oxygen from each breath than they would if they had only lungs. Pilots have observed migrating geese, serenely flying at their usual cruising speed of forty-five miles an hour, over the Himalaya Mountains at altitudes of 30,000 feet, where oxygen is a third that at sea level. Wind and weather permitting, the parula we were looking at may have taken off from Central Park after dark that same day and moved on another 200 miles nearer to its breeding ground, the northernmost edge of which lies in the forests of eastern Canada, a couple of thousand miles from Yucatán.

Resuming our climb up the slope, we soon discovered four other warblers: a yellowthroat, in an alder, trilling its *witchety-witchety* call; a Louisiana water thrush, a warbler despite its name; the ovenbird ("A plump warbler that dwells on the ground. Rather confusing, that," said Keith); and a myrtle, the only warbler that sometimes winters in this area, subsisting principally on bayberries and poison-ivy berries. "Hear its song?" Keith said. "It always sounds as if it wasn't giving it all it could."

Keith suddenly turned 180 degrees and put his glasses on a cluster of viburnum. "Ah," he said. "Getting a little action here." A wood thrush was in the branches, and on the ground below was a brown thrasher, a red-brown bird nearly a foot long—really a mockingbird—that possesses one of birddom's more beautiful songs. "The Ramble, with its water and high and low vegetation, is just the sort of place these thrush-like birds seek," said Keith. Below dogwood and inkberry hung with white flowers, the thrasher scuttled over a rubble of dank newspapers, candy wrappers, cigarette packs, and trampled paper cups, typical terrain, unfortunately, in some parts of the Park.

I heard a cheep. "Ah!" I said. "A new note."

"Ah, getting a little action here."

"An English sparrow," said Keith. "The commonest bird in the Park, I'm afraid. That and the starling or pigeon."

Some yards farther on, near the Ramble's crest, high up in a tall ash tree by the trickling Gill, we sighted a robin's nest, fashioned by migrants that may have come from no farther south than Philadelphia. As we looked, a parent returned and four small heads popped above the rim. That was the only occupied nest we saw, but about twenty species have been observed nesting regularly or occasionally in the Park during the past decade, most of them in the Ramble. A dozen or so are generally found in any one year. Since nesting records began to be kept for the Park, more than eighty years ago, nearly fifty species have been known to breed there. The number of nesting birds depends in part on the amount of shrubbery, which had recently been kept to a minimum to discourage muggings.

It was now after ten o'clock. Human activity in the Ramble began to pick up. Nursemaids with children appeared. Commercial dog-walkers, in some cases tugged far off the vertical by their charges, pounded across the walks. On the Lake, two young oarsmen in full breeding plumage (long hair, bell-bottomed trousers, heavy chain necklaces with pendants) maneuvered their rowboats to ram one another while their female passengers joyously made counterfeit alarm noises. Other bird-watchers passed us, singly and in groups. A party of elderly ladies was hearing one member expound, with enormous satisfaction, the etymology of the word "redstart," the name of a warbler: "'*Staart*' is Dutch for 'tail.' Thus 'redtail'—'redstart.'"

Above the ladies, a gray squirrel scuttled noisily over branches near the top of a lofty oak. Keith regarded it unenthusiastically. "Human feeding keeps the population at an artificially high level here," he said. The squirrel entered a large, dilapidated wooden box, one of several such creations visible in the Ramble, all in rather poor repair. A German woman was their architect. For a number of years, before she returned to her homeland after the Second World War, she used to bedevil the Park gardeners—under threat of letters to the newspapers charging neglect of animals—to build and place the structures as shelters for what she said were the Ramble's otherwise unsheltered squirrels.

"Aha! What have we here?" said Keith, taking his gaze from the oak and concentrating narrowly on a thick privet shrub some yards off. "Get that thrush? Either a Swainson's or a gray-cheek—both fairly common. A Swainson's, I think. But don't put it down. It eluded me." Thus challenged, he approached the shrub, very alert, and, with his fist to his lips, made low, squeaking, birdlike sounds—a tactic that often proves irresistible to even the shyest birds, who, upon hearing it, will show themselves to find out what's going on. Sure enough, before long a Swainson's thrush poked its head up, and was duly noted.

In quick succession, we acquired three fine warblers—all, of course, spotted by Keith. "Whoops! A black-throated blue," he said of a bird in a spicebush. "Though not one of the top fifteen, fairly rare." In a hornbeam just beyond was a Wilson's, a bright-yellow bird with a black cap, which Keith called "one of the less numerous ones." Both were males, and very colorful. (Even in spring, the female warblers tend to be more sombre.) Almost instantly thereafter, we chanced on a notably elusive bird, the mourning warbler. "Well," Keith said, with satisfaction, and lowered his glasses. Looking where he pointed, I saw, slinking about the lowest branches of a mock-orange bush some ten yards off, a black-bibbed, yellow-breasted, olive-backed mite of a bird. "Very sneaky. Hard to see, that one. Crouches in very low shrubs. A skulker."

A bit farther on, as we descended toward the Lake, three pigeons rose from a ginkgo, providing a mundane addition to our list. A true urban resident, New York's pigeon is a run-down variant of a proud stock known as the European rock dove, which also produced the racing pigeon. The racing pigeon can move faster on its own power alone than any other creature; in level flight it can reach speeds of nearly a hundred miles an hour. Overhead, its lumpen cousins flapped about lazily.

We now left the Ramble, crossing between the cast-iron sides of Bow Bridge—so called for its graceful, slightly arched shape—toward Cherry Hill, a rise to the south of the Lake. On our way, we passed a turkey oak in whose branches one memorable day in May some years back a single observer spotted no fewer than forty species of migrants. At the moment, the tree was bare of birds. So, by and large, was Cherry Hill, the lone exception being a starling occupying a nesting hole in the trunk of a tulip tree which Keith believed to have been originally made by redheaded woodpeckers.

We picked up a few more birds while we wandered about Azalea Pond, back in the Ramble. A little past the Rustic Bridge, we came on a large European white birch whose thick trunk was pitted with rows of deep parallel depressions, made, according to Keith, by the yellow-bellied sapsucker on its spring and fall migrations. The bird drills the holes and then returns both to drink the sap and to eat the insects that have been attracted to it. Three ragged teen-agers who skidded to a stop behind us seemed puzzled by the regular pattern of holes. But one of them quickly provided an explanation. Pointing an imaginary shoulder gun at the tree, he went, "Bang, bang! Shotgun, man!" All three were instantly off again, running low through the shrubbery.

Keith told me that he started birding at the age of sixteen—the result of a gift from his parents of an excellent pair of binoculars. He has continued it uninterruptedly ever since. During a tour of duty in the Far East with the King's Own Scottish Borderers, he would spend his off-duty hours in Korea and in Hong Kong's New Territories watching Asiatic buntings, which he described as "akin to your sparrows." His North American bird record of 594 species, by which he dethroned Roger Tory Peterson, one of the most famous of contemporary ornithologists, stood for fifteen years, but now no longer stands. Since 1971, four persons, lucky enough to get most of the birds on Keith's list and some others such as Swainson's warbler and the great gray owl, which he missed, have come up with totals of over 600 species, acquired, as was the case with Keith, by putting in twelve often arduous months and travelling some 50,000 or more miles, at times under primitive conditions. However, Keith has since gone on to greater ornithological glory. From North American champion, he has now become world champion with a life list that surpasses 4,550 species. Keith is thus the only person living or dead to have seen more than half of the earth's approximately 8,800 bird species.

In order to fatten our own list for the day, we left the Ramble and moved north to see what water birds were at the Reservoir. On the way, we walked under an arbor of Chinese wisteria heavy with grapelike clusters of purple flowers, and past a stretch of greensward known as Burns Lawn, which bore a haze of azure scilla flowers that Keith said put him in mind of bluebells in a British spring. As we came in sight of the Winterdale Arch, which spans the bridle path, the sound of some furious birds' billingsgate made us look up. Five grackles were chasing a broad-winged hawk toward the Beresford Apartments, at the corner of Central Park West and Eighty-first Street, hurling epithets and making aerial passes at it. The hawk had apparently lost its way on migration. Normally, the variety moves to the west in large flocks over a route above the Ramapo Mountains, in New Jersey, a more westerly part of the Atlantic Flyway.

"Poor broadwings," said Keith. "They always get it from the grackles."

Although broadwings prefer a diet of rodents, the grackles chased this one as avidly as if it were a notorious nest robber like a crow, leaving off only when their target had cleared the building's roof.

"They wouldn't do that if the duck hawks were still there," I said. The duck hawk—or peregrine falcon, as it is usually called these days—is an unrelenting bird-eater with a wingspan of more than a yard, at whose sight the grackles would have quietly taken to the trees. Back in 1948, the Beresford Apartments—twenty-two stories crowned by three squat towers—provided a perch for a rather famous pair of peregrines, which used to dive on quarry, mostly pigeons, over the Park. Usually the pigeons were too slow-moving to make the birds exert themselves, but a peregrine, often starting its swoop with quick wingbeats, can drop like a thunderbolt, reaching speeds of 180 miles an hour, and kills its prey with clenched talons. Before 1948, this same pair had frequented other tall buildings in midtown. One spring morning in 1943, an elderly lady who occupied a suite on the sixteenth floor of the Hotel St. Regis complained of noise outside her window. A housekeeper who was sent to investigate opened the balcony's French windows and immediately wished she hadn't for she had intruded upon an aerie that the two peregrines had established there. Eventually, the A.S.P.C.A. sent a suitably armored contingent to take the young away. Although breeding was rare in Manhattan, at least a dozen other peregrines were seen in the 1940s.

"Why are there no more around?" I asked Keith.

"One factor certainly seems to be pesticides,"

he said. "These get into the eggs through the food chain, often rendering them infertile."

When we reached the Reservoir, we stopped at about the level of Eighty-eighth Street, and Keith put his glasses on the water, coming up with some ring-billed, great black-backed, and herring gulls. All of them were immature, the older birds of those species being normally at their coastal nesting grounds by that time of year. But he also spotted one mature laughing gull.

It was then about eleven-thirty in the morning. Totting up the list of species we had seen, we found we had forty-one, seventeen of them warblers. "Not good. But not bad," said Keith. They comprised, besides the ones already mentioned, the following warblers —the bay-breasted, black-and-white, black-throated green, Canada, chestnut-sided, and magnolia, along with the northern water thrush, redstart, and yellow-breasted chat (the largest warbler). The remaining thrushes were the gray-cheeked and the veery, and rounding out the list were the catbird, red-winged blackbird, wood pewee, white-throated sparrow (a laggard), house wren, goldfinch, blue jay, and some white Pekin ducks swimming in front of the boathouse. The record for birds seen in Central Park on one day is ninety-nine species, set in 1954 by several dozen observers fanned out across the Park. That was the occasion of the turkey oak's moment of glory, and one for the Atlantic Flyway, as well.

2
Meteorite Man

Also hanging high above Central Park are features of
the sky more distant than the Atlantic Flyway—the
stars, the planets, and their various celestial companions. Admittedly, as night descends upon the town,
these outriders of our globe, owing to the interference
of a frequently polluted atmosphere and the glare of
lights within and without the Park, are often as invisible to city dwellers as the vaporous boundaries of the
Flyway. However, on clear nights, as the hours roll past
midnight and some of the lights of the city dim, a resident standing on an apartment terrace overlooking
the Park can sometimes see night's silvery embroidery

17

at its most splendid. Stars with a tinge of reddish, blue, or green color, a planet or two as well, perhaps, and the moon may be on view. Also, if the occasion takes place during certain months, especially August or November, the watcher may observe the sparkle of meteor showers cascading down the inky wall of night like dizzy driblets of diamond chips.

If, for the sake of simplicity, we discount the billions of stars that float in the ether around us and limit ourselves to a consideration of what lies in the still enormous reaches of the solar system, we find, apart from the sun, the major member, that this space is occupied by five categories of objects—the planets, their satellites, the asteroids, comets, and meteoroids. We shall confine our attention to the last.

As long as meteoroids remain in space, science calls them by that one name, meteoroids. As soon as they enter the earth's atmosphere, however, they are divided into two different categories, meteors and meteorites. Meteors are the things people commonly call "shooting stars." Meteorites are larger pieces of matter that fall from space onto the earth.

The second-largest meteorite so far known, and the largest ever recovered and put on public display, is the thirty-six ton specimen mounted in the lobby of the Seventy-seventh Street entrance of the American Museum of Natural History just west of the Park. It was brought from its resting place on Cape York in Greenland early this century under the direction of Admiral Peary. In discussing it with museum officials not too many months ago, I learned of a scientist, with whom I shortly visited.

He is a man most people would certainly say possesses a singular gift. For he can tell at a glance the stones that fall from the heavens from those that are born of the earth. These sky stones, as the man in the street sometimes calls them, are meteorites, and the scientist I talked with has been their collector, admirer, and student for most of his professional life of more than half a century. He is Dr. Edward P. Henderson, and he so esteems, respects, and empathizes with meteorites, at present those still largely mysterious missiles which, unknown and unseen by most of the public, ceaselessly bombard our planet, that he might well be called their friend. A necessary preliminary to his work, of course, is their identification. "You recognize them after a while almost by instinct," he told me as we sat during my visit in his office in the Smithsonian Institution in Washington, D.C. "The eye becomes critical. For meteorites are heavier . . . they have a different structure . . . than earth rocks. To the initiate they appear to be quite apart from them. It's like having a built-in scanning computer."

In the more than forty years that he has been at the Smithsonian studying meteorites, eventually as the curator of its rather recently established Division of Meteorites, Henderson has examined hundreds of objects of both terrestrial and celestial origin from all of the fifty states and a dozen foreign countries, the items often being accompanied by their finders. "Usually I can tell yes or no merely by lifting the unopened package," Henderson said. "Once it is unwrapped, however, there is never any doubt. Meteorites that have just come down and are known in scientific terminology as fresh falls are covered wholly or in part with a smooth skin. Normally this is black, but sometimes it is lighter colored, and occasionally even white, depending on the meteorite's composition. The skin is acquired in the journey through the atmosphere that takes place at many miles a second. The friction burns off some of the exterior causing the trail of fire seen at night and often in the daytime. With big meteorites, the light at night may be so intense as to cast shadows within an area 400 miles in diameter. In the lower atmosphere the meteorites slow down and the melt solidifies. It is very thin, a matter of a millimeter or so. Fresh falls are not redhot, as legend sometimes has it, for the interior of the meteorite is never heated. At most, it is slightly warm. Meteorites that are located after their descent we refer to as finds. They normally lack the smooth skin and generally are weathered because many have come down hundreds or even thousands of years ago. They resemble to a considerable degree terrestrial rocks, especially sandstone. Usually they are rusty brown in appearance. Recognizing them is where the computer eye comes in."

About ten meteorites of highly varying size are estimated to drop on this country each year. But only a small percentage is recovered; actually, there have been less than ten in the last decade. The Smithsonian receives, however, twenty-five to thirty letters each month reporting, mostly erroneously, meteorite discoveries and, in addition, literally hundreds of letters and excited telephone calls during the spectacular shooting-star displays that regularly occur at certain specific times. Nevertheless, despite the high percentage of incorrect leads, Henderson and the Smithsonian adopt a positive attitude toward meteorite recovery. The Institution answers all the letters meticulously, receives the telephone calls politely, and Henderson himself is constantly on the lookout for meteorites wherever he goes. As a matter of fact, in 1964 and 1965, when he was curator of the division he traveled halfway around the world with Dr. Brian Mason, the present curator, to look for meteorites in the flat, dry interior of Australia, an optimum locale for their recovery. Proceeding by Land Rover to likely spots and then searching assiduously on foot, the two men came up with dozens of specimens. It is one of the bright memories of Henderson's life.

Henderson, who is a ruddy, white-haired, spectacled individual of seventy-five, has been, since 1966, curator emeritus. Instead of getting to his office, as had long been his custom, at quarter to seven in the morning, six days a week, and working until four in the afternoon, he now curtails this schedule a bit. But a year or two ago, he went back to Australia to ferret out more meteorites. In 1971, he was awarded the J. Lawrence Smith Medal by the National Academy of Sciences for his investigation of meteoric bodies, the sixth time the honor has been bestowed since its inception early in this century, when J. Lawrence Smith, a chemist, left a sum of money to the Academy for an award to an outstanding student of meteorites. Mostly under Henderson's long stewardship, the meteorite collection at the Smithsonian has risen from 400 to more than 1,330 specimens, placing it first in the world, ahead of the collections in such notable institutions as the British Museum, the Natural History Museum of Paris, and the Vienna Natural History Museum.

Meteorites and their smaller cousins, the meteors, come from space within the solar system, a region that is large but far from empty. Standing outdoors any night in clear air in the country and watching a restricted portion of the sky, a person with average vision can see during an hour or so an average of from twenty to sixty "shooting stars," the common term for meteors. With the aid of a high-powered telescope, the number may be increased a thousand times. The infall continues, of course, day and night. Occasional increases in it have been known to make people fear for their lives as well as for the planet's security. One such occasion was the night of November 13, 1833. Frightened Bostonians fell to their knees, imploring God's pity on themselves and the environment and, in addition, asking for a postponement of the Day of Judgment, which they felt was surely arriving. Over them, for many hours in the sky, meteors seemed thick as snowflakes in a winter storm—although, actually, scientists know today, that they were probably ten to fifteen miles apart. Lesser increases in meteor infall occur periodically each year, the greatest normally being in mid-August, when the earth's orbit for about five days swings through the Perseids, a cloud of finely divided interplanetary matter, bits and pieces of which speckle clear nighttime skies during the interval with incessant prickles of light. They arrive on the order of fifty visible to the naked eye an hour.

Most meteors are believed to be roughly the size of grains of sand. They ignite during their descent, giving off the lines of light that mark part of their passage through the atmosphere. The light comes from the kindling of the meteor's external molecules by atmospheric friction and their constant detachment during descent. Usually the light is white. But red, green, and yellow have also been observed. The ratio of the meteor's matter to the amount of the light produced has been estimated to be that of a football to a football field. Occasionally, in daylight falls, a trail of smoke is noted. The trail is thought, like that of terrestrial smoke, to consist of partly burnt particles. Apparently, from telescopic observation of meteors, there is virtually no limit to their tininess. The material that will eventually cause the smallest shooting stars is thought, as it floats high up in the atmosphere, to produce the zodiacal light, the nebulous glow seen in the west after sunset and in the east before dawn. Presumably, it is the reflection of the sun's light from these wee specks hanging miles over the earth.

On the other hand, meteors can be much larger than the usual sand-grain size. Pieces of matter ten to twenty pounds in weight, it is estimated, can be transformed through incandescence into visible light and feathery ash as they traverse the atmosphere. The light of meteors is extinguished five to ten miles above the earth, and the consequent residue floats slowly to earth, invisible to the naked eye. These meteoric remnants, astronomers think, represent the bulk of the 3,000 tons of interplanetary material that is calculated to rain in daily on the earth.

The rest of this material is meteorites. Meteorites and meteoric ash are the only things from interplanetary space that in historic times are known to have reached the earth in ponderable form.

Comets, which are other wanderers in interplanetary space, zoom about the sun in highly irregular orbits, often seen once and never again. Their heads, which can be formidably large (a matter of many thousands of miles), are believed to be composed of meteoroids of various sizes apparently stuck together with frozen gases. When comets swing near the sun, its radiation vaporizes some of the gases, which then stream out before or behind the head, depending on whether it is approaching or leaving our luminary. The result produces glowing tails often many millions of miles in length. Solar radiation also sometimes breaks up some, or all, of the comet. When this occurs, the meteoroids freed in the process become the potential nuclei for forming another comet.

The final category of interplanetary material,

apart from the planets themselves and their satellites, are the asteroids. These could, technically speaking, be included in the general term of meteoroids. But because of their large size they are usually kept apart. Most of them are believed to be circulating in rather irregular orbits in the space between Mars and Jupiter. Scientists think they are either the result of the breakup of a planet or pieces that have not agglomerated into one. Millions, measuring a yard or more in size, are thought to be moving in this region, and some 1,600 have been catalogued and tracked. The largest, named Ceres, is almost 500 miles in diameter; Vesta, somewhat smaller, is, because of its proximity to earth, the only one visible to the naked eye. Perturbations of asteroid orbit caused by the gravitational influences of Mars and Jupiter operating over the cycles of cosmological time have doubtless tossed many out of these paths to travel elsewhere in the solar system, but the number is not known. Seen through a telescope, the asteroids in the belt display a highly varying luminosity, one that can change from hour to hour, a circumstance that would follow if, as astronomers believe, the asteroids are highly irregular bodies tumbling through space and reflecting the sun's radiation from surfaces now flat, now jagged, now thin, now thick.

Irregularity of form is also a trait shared by the meteorites. They come to earth utterly nondescript. Some are cone- or leaf-shaped. Shells, turtles, doughnuts, pears, jawbones, and bells are other objects to which they have been compared. Many have squarish angles. A number are pitted where the heat of atmospheric passage has consumed material softer than that adjoining. None has been known to arrive as a sphere. Diversity in the direction of flight is another characteristic. Both meteors and meteorites come into the atmosphere from almost any direction overhead. Meteorites in particular seem to have highly sporadic patterns.

The earth, scientists believe, is made of a core of nickel-iron covered by layers of molten and solid rock, a reckoning that is based on its weight in comparison to its size. The weight is arrived at by computing the effect of the earth's gravitational pull on other celestial objects. By the same method, Mercury and Venus, on the sunward side of the earth, and Mars in the other direction just beyond it, also seem to be made of rock and iron. So do the asteroids.

This composition is quite different from that of the larger planets—Jupiter, Saturn, Uranus, and Neptune. They apparently consist of heavily packed condensations of the very lightest elements and their compounds. (Pluto, the planet farthest from earth, is far too tiny and remote for astronomers to have reached any firm conclusions about its makeup.)

Meteorites, in contrast to the larger planets, are known to consist of exactly what the rock-and-iron planets are thought to consist of, namely, rock and nickel-iron. More than 90 percent of the meteorites recovered have been found to be of stony material. This is much like the crust of the earth. These meteorites are known colloquially by scientists as stones. The next largest category, a figure of more than 5 percent of the recovered meteorites, consists of a mixture of nickel-iron, the presumptive material at the core of the earth. These are known as irons. The remainder, less than 2 percent, are called the stony irons, being usually an equal mixture of the two materials. Furthermore, meteors, those objects that do not reach the earth in original form, when examined by the spectroscope (a gadget that tells scientists what's in a bright or glowing object) also are found to be stones.

The study of meteorites had a decidedly delayed start in the annals of science. While other branches of knowledge such as chemistry and physics were laying solid foundations 300 or 400 years ago, that of meteorites was unborn. In fact, even the existence of meteorites was widely doubted until relatively recently. A remark by Thomas Jefferson illustrates this. In 1808, Yale Professors Silliman and Kingsley announced that a meteorite had fallen at Weston, Connecticut, a fact that was duly reported to Jefferson, then the President. "It's easier to believe two Yankee professors would lie than that stones would fall from heaven," Jefferson declared. The work of the German physicist, Chaldni, published in 1794, on which the science of meteorites is based, had not yet gained general acceptance. An early convert, however, was James Smithson, the founder of the Smithsonian Institution. Smithson, the natural son of the Duke of Northumberland and the wealthy Elizabeth Keats Macie, herself a direct descendant of King Henry VII of England, was one of the first collectors of meteorites. He amassed his collection during his stay in Europe at the beginning of the last century. The collection was brought to this country when the Smithsonian was founded in 1846, but it and Smithson's data concerning it perished in the organization's disastrous fire of 1865. In the light of Smithson's interest, it may be fitting that through the efforts of Henderson and others the Institution he created now has parts of, or the whole of, the majority of the 1,800-odd meteorites that have been known to have been retrieved to date.

Among the Smithsonian specimens are the six falls recorded in the United States in the last seven years— one each from New York, Oklahoma, Connecticut, and California, and two from Colorado. The New York fall occurred at Schenectady on the evening of April 12, 1968. It was observed by some twenty persons, who reported its course as coming from the zenith. The meteorite, a stone of about half a pound, splintered a portion of the eaves of a house and rebounded onto the ground, where it was found. It had a dull, black fusion crust and a fracture surface indicating a breakup in the atmosphere.

Three percent, a fairly large number, of recovered falls have struck buildings. The preceding one in this country, which came down in Colorado in July of the year previous to the Schenectady fall, was actually found because of this circumstance. It was another stone of about the same size as the Schenectady one, and it punctured the roof of a warehouse in Denver. The resultant investigation of the cause of a leak disclosed the object on the roof lying near the break. Despite this fairly frequent building damage, only one person in this country is known to have been struck by a meteorite. That was a widow in Sylacauga, Alabama, in 1954. She was resting on a couch when a stone of about eight pounds came through the roof of her house and struck her on the thigh, leaving a watermelon-sized bruise. *Life* magazine shortly printed a picture of this.

A recent fall, at Lost City, Oklahoma, in January 1970, was acquired through the workings of the Smithsonian's Photographic Meteorite Recovery Program, set up in 1964 under Henderson's curatorship. Sixteen unmanned, fully automatic camera stations are located in the flat, treeless Middle West, a likely region for spotting or finding incoming celestial objects. The network, whose positions are approximately 160 miles apart, ranges from South Dakota to Oklahoma and from Illinois to Nebraska. All night the cameras take pictures every few seconds of an allotted portion of the sky. Since, when an object's path is spotted by three or more cameras, its trajectory can be plotted and perhaps its landing place as well, the network is the Smithsonian's newest hope of increasing its meteorite collection. Prior to January, 1970, the paths of four presumptive meteorites had been plotted, but none recovered.

In that month, however, following the trail of one that had been observed by the cameras, a network employee, driving along a lonely, one-track road covered by four inches of snow, some sixty miles east of Tulsa, where it had been predicted the end point would be, passed a twenty-two-pound black stone lying at the road's edge. After proceeding a few yards, the man did a double-take and backed up to examine it. The black fusion crust sent him into a happy delirium. Less than a day later, at 4 A.M., at Friendship Airport outside Washington, five of Henderson's colleagues met the stone and its finder with excited gabblings. Henderson viewed the object at a quarter to seven that morning. A fortunate feature of the discovery was the stone's landing on a public road. This obviated negotiation with a landowner. By the Antiquities Act, Public Law 209, passed by Congress on June 8, 1906, objects in this country considered national treasures are government property when found on public land. Meteorites are considered national treasures, a country road is public land, and the Smithsonian is a government institution. Meteorites on private land, however, are the property of the owner. They are acquired, usually but not always, with a minimum of difficulty through negotiation, ending in purchase. Prices fluctuate, depending on the owner's personality and the size and condition of the specimen, but usually they range from a few dollars to several hundred.

The Connecticut fall occurred in April, 1971, in Wethersfield, a stony meteorite of better than three-quarters of a pound, striking the roof of the house of Mr. and Mrs. Paul Cassarino and almost penetrating through the ceiling of a room on an upper floor. The California fall, on March 15, 1973, also struck a building. A small stone, weighing about two ounces, punctured the aluminum roof of a carport in San Juan Capistrano.

The latest fall, as we go to press, descended on Canyon City, Colorado, on October 27, 1973. The meteorite, a stone of over three pounds, also pierced a roof, an untypical fifth of six falls to hit one.

Meteoroids have a cosmic velocity of their own, its rate depending on the speed of their orbit around the sun. They are drawn out of orbit and toward the earth by the power of its gravitation, taking fire high in the atmosphere. Luminosity begins about ninety miles up. There the air is thin but dense enough to start incandescence through friction.

Depending on the size and composition of the meteoroid, its subsequent career varies. A medium-sized object weighing several hundred pounds crackles and rumbles in descent. The sounds, as many as a dozen in number during the flight, which lasts from a few to a score of seconds, accompany the creation of surface fractures due to rapid heating or atmospheric shearing stress. Onlookers within earshot have compared what they hear to rifle shots. The noises are more or less numerous and intense depending on the nature of the aerial contention. Sonic booms also may accompany them. The earth travels around the sun at a speed of more than eighteen miles a second, carrying the atmosphere with it. The battle is sharpest when the meteoroid collides head on with the atmosphere moving in an opposite direction. But all meteoroids, no matter what their angle of approach, fight with the atmosphere and are somewhat diminished by it, the lost material spalling off in pieces, or departing as vaporized gas or fiery droplets.

In the case of a medium-sized meteoroid, air resistance eventually slows it till the point of retardation is reached five to twenty miles above the earth's surface. There, the column of air packed down by the incoming meteoroid is so compressed, highly heated, and full of energy that an explosion occurs, bursting the meteoroid—more thoroughly if it is a stone or stony iron, less so if it is an iron. Observers then hear a noise like a cannon's blast, shortly followed by a second one, as the displaced air readjusts itself. These sound effects cause meteorites in some rural areas to be called thunderstones, a name that has a venerable past. One of the first meteorites noted (in the Parian Chronicle) as falling in the western world, came down on the island of Crete about 1478 B.C., and was described as a thunderstone.

When the explosion at the point of retardation takes place, incandescence ceases, the smooth fusion crust solidifies, and the pieces fall to earth with their cosmic velocity obliterated. The pieces drop then under the force of gravity alone, as would any objects falling from that height. Normally, observers hear the sounds at proper intervals following the light phenomena that accompany the burst. Light, of course, travels at the speed of electromagnetic radiation, which is much faster than that of sound. But the conventional sequence is not always the case. Many observers over the years have reported simultaneous reception of light and sound. The anomaly is evidently the result of objects in the vicinity of the observer transforming the electromagnetic waves into true sound waves. This sometimes happens under other circumstances also. A recent example, cited by the British General Practitioners Association, reported a Florida housewife's teeth broadcasting music, the teeth evidently turning the electromagnetic radio waves somehow into sound waves.

Meteoroids destined to become small meteorites (in the general range of fist-sized pieces) undergo the same entry process as that described for the somewhat larger ones, the main difference being that the atmosphere decelerates them more quickly. Meteoroids of twenty pounds or under never become meteorites, but burn up as meteors in the atmosphere.

Large meteoroids of several tons or more, however, act differently. They are not halted by the air. Some reduction in size occurs through friction and spalling, but the mass remains far greater than that of the atmosphere through which it punches. Thus it approaches earth at a speed of many miles a second. Upon striking the ground, the enormous kinetic energy of its velocity is changed in the twinkling of an eye to that of heat. The physics of the collision requires that virtually all the mass of the incoming object (and much of the material, too, in the area in which it strikes) be converted almost instantaneously into gas. This, of course, causes an explosion. A crater is formed whose rim and outside perimeter are sprinkled with bits and pieces of that relatively small fraction of the meteorite escaping vaporization. But to all intents and purposes the once huge hunk of interplanetary matter has vanished.

The largest meteorite known lies in a pit in Southwest Africa, an object known as the Hoba iron, measuring nine feet by nine feet by three and one-quarter feet, and weighing an estimated sixty-six tons.

Throughout history primitive peoples have believed that meteorites, having fallen from the sky, are sacred gifts of the gods. This was the case with the American Museum of Natural History's iron that Admiral Peary brought back from Greenland. The Eskimos told him (erroneously, as it turned out) that the iron's removal would have dire consequences for him. The famous Black Stone embedded in the wall of the Kaaba, the small stone building in the court of the Great Mosque at Mecca, is thought to be another such instance. The stone, which Henderson suspects is a meteorite, has had a history of worship long antedating the founding of Islam by Mohammed. "I made a little study of this matter years ago," Henderson told me. "Mohammed from the beginning seemed a different sort from his fellows. He constantly harangued against the worship of the idols made by man at the Kaaba, even then a holy place, in his home town of Mecca. The merchants, of course, resented this. The idols brought many pilgrims. Finally, in A.D. 623, Mohammed had to flee for his life. In A.D. 630, when he returned to Mecca as its conqueror from a city to the north, he threw out all the man-made idols in the Kaaba. But he kept the Black Stone, which was not made by man. Legend far older than Mohammed had recorded the stone as falling from heaven. Most likely it fell near Mecca, probably with the usual noise and light phenomena, which convinced the finders that its descent was supernatural. Today the faithful are asked to kiss or touch it with a finger on each of the seven required circumambulations of the Kaaba, a small, almost cubical, stone structure. When crowds before the Black Stone are too dense, touching it with a stick is permitted. It pleases me that the object seen and touched by more people than any other in the world, as well as the cause of probably the world's greatest traffic jams, is in all likelihood a meteorite." But the establishment beyond dispute of this highly venerated object's meteoric origin is, Henderson admits, one of the unlikeliest eventualities facing science because of unquestioned Moslem resistance that would arise to any tests, chemical or otherwise, on the stone.

The largest stone meteorite that has been retrieved so far fell in Kansas in 1948. It weighed 2,000 pounds and is the largest meteorite of any kind recovered from an observed fall. The oldest known fall is an iron that was struck by an oil drill in 1940 in Zapata County, Texas. It was some 500 feet below the surface, embedded in rock strata of the Eocene epoch, laid down about 40 million years ago.

Some three dozen large craters are now known to science as being definitely of meteoritic origin. The largest and best preserved of these is the Barringer crater near Winslow, Arizona. It is almost a mile across and 600 feet deep below the rim which, in turn, rises to 223 feet above the surrounding terrain. The crater's true floor, however, which has become overlaid with detritus, is 600 to 800 feet lower, arguing that it was formed perhaps 50,000 years ago by a great piece of iron, some fragments of which have been picked up in the rim and outside. The next largest crater, about two-thirds as wide, is in Australia and is known as Wolf Creek, around which Henderson found a number of stony irons. (Larger unconfirmed craters are, among others, the Chubb Crater in northern Quebec, almost circular and nearly two miles across, discovered in 1950 during aerial reconnaissance, and the Vreedefort Ring Structure of South Africa, some twenty-four miles in diameter.)

No immense masses of matter capable of forming such craters have been known for a certainty to have fallen in historic times. This is fortunate. A hit by one on a city would severely damage or wipe it out. However, one possible exception exists. On the morning of June 30, 1908, in swampy ground near the Tunguska River in north central Siberia something extraordinary unquestionably happened. Science is not sure at this point just exactly what. People reported seeing an incoming fireball brighter than the sun. Forty miles from the apparent point of impact a peasant was blown from his porch. Tremors were widely felt. Water gushed spontaneously from the earth in many places. Dwellings twenty to thirty miles distant were shaken down. Lakes and streams showed tidal movements. Barographs as far away as London recorded an aerial disturbance.

Not until almost twenty years later, in 1927, did an investigation team from Moscow reach the general area. They viewed a strange sight. For twenty miles around one spot all trees were flattened, their tops missing, their trunks pointing outward from a common center like a forest of felled telephone poles. The investigators were unable to pinpoint precisely the exact point of impact. Nor did they find a true crater. Nor any meteorite fragments.

Science now thinks one of three things happened.

For twenty miles, all trees were flattened,
their tops missing.

A great meteorite buried itself in the earth, the resultant crater and meteorite remains being obscured as
the swampy terrain readjusted itself over the years.
The second thought is that a great stony mass exploded
in the air over the land, blowing down the trees in the
observed symmetrical fashion and causing the other
effects. The third suggestion, which has an eerie quality, is that an event of an as yet unknown nature occurred.

Henderson, who started his career as a geochemist
with the Geological Survey of the Department of the Interior, came to the Smithsonian's Department of Geology in 1930 at the age of thirty-one, following the
death of the head of the department, Dr. George P.
Merrill, who had served the Smithsonian forty-three

years, a record that Henderson has now surpassed. Although Merrill directed a general geology department, he was interested in, and worked almost exclusively with, meteorites. On Henderson's arrival, since none of the rest of the staff cared about meteorites, the job was handed to him. For years he did it alone. However, when he retired at the end of 1966 as curator of the newly formed Division of Meteorites, organized in 1963, the scientific staff had grown to six, one fewer than it has at the moment.

Henderson from the beginning followed the lines laid down by Merrill, whose aim was to increase scientific accuracy in the examination of meteorites. Over the years under Henderson, X-ray and chemical-analysis laboratories were gradually installed, along with petrographs for the scrutiny and classification of rocky material, electron microprobes for determining structure without cleavage, and cutting and polishing facilities—all with this purpose in mind.

But perhaps Henderson's greatest achievement, even more than his procurement of hardware, was his ability to acquire meteorites from the populace at large. Numerous letters were sent to the Smithsonian about meteorites and the writers invariably received extensive replies from Henderson. Those who brought in actual objects, whether meteorites or not, were given his undivided attention for as long as they wished to stay. "When a fellow talks about meteorites, either in person or on paper, we are prepared to listen to him," Henderson told me. He has travelled in every state in the Union, tracking down suspected quarry, and during his journeys, as in his letters and interviews, he has never failed assiduously to seek converts to his cause, speaking in local schools, to newspaper staffs, and natural history society members about how to search for, and recognize, meteorites and, when found, where to send them. In this way he built up a network of informers and potential informers whose numbers eventually approximated a small army. He is always enthusiastic. Once in a little town in Georgia, after having acquired a handsome iron, he was so inspired that he poked around in a plowed field nearby and came up with another. Practically nobody who, to Henderson's knowledge, has ever possessed a meteorite has been able, ultimately, to deny it to him. "This man is a real bulldog," one of his colleagues admiringly said.

Henderson views his professional life, still highly energetic, as an eminently happy one. "It involves travel, adventure, scientific problems, and as much finagling as any businessman's. Who could want more than that?" he said to me. One of his better pieces of finagling was gaining the friendship of the late Stuart H. Perry, whose relations with Merrill had been fairly cool. Perry, a wealthy newspaper publisher in Michigan, a vice president of the Associated Press, and, ultimately, the fourth recipient of the J. Lawrence Smith Medal, was an amateur meteorite collector and a virtual fanatic on the subject, owning, after several decades of activity, one of the largest collections in private hands. By the time of his death in 1957 most of this, amounting to approximately 100 items, had come to the Smithsonian through the influence of Henderson.

Henderson's ability to finagle—or ever to maneuver in the direction of more meteorites—is also reflected in his trading proficiency. As curator, he wrote indefatigably to individuals, universities, and other museums owning meteorites that the Smithsonian did not have, offering slices of those in his hands for parts in possession of his correspondents, a program that was notably successful. (For example, Henderson estimates that Perry's gifts over the years produced six times their own number.)

Toward the end of my visit, Henderson and I took a tour of the meteorite department, almost all of which is located near his office on the fourth floor of the Smithsonian building known as the National Museum of Natural History. We passed through various rooms occupied by technical apparatus, some of which was being used by staff members, and paused longer than usual in one that contained a back-to-back double row of gray steel filing cabinets reaching almost to the ceiling. On the drawer fronts were printed labels, in back of which were stored most of the Smithsonian's meteorites. These normally bear titles indicating their place of discovery. Many were bizarre names, some in abstruse languages, such as Akota, Braunau, Jelica, Knyahinga, Mocs, Nakhla, New Concord, and Sikhote-Alin. Index cards alphabetically arranged by name, like those in libraries, were there in another set of files, giving the location of the meteorites in the cabinets. A final set of files contained a collection of photographs of them.

Care is required to preserve meteorites. They come from a region of virtually constant temperature and pressure. The exceedingly tenuous gas in space offers small opportunity for alterations through chemical activity. In space they remain (it is thought) almost exactly as they have been for billions of years. The situation on earth is different. Temperature here is far from constant, pressure quite different from that of space, and our relatively rich atmosphere with its highly reactive oxygen and water is capable of inducing chemical changes that would not be possible in space. All specimens therefore, whether stored or displayed, must be given a coat of protective lacquer as soon as possible, after first having been thoroughly cleaned of dust and lint. In addition, those on display must be shown in cases with as little temperature and light change as may be managed. Neglect of these rules causes on the meteorite's exterior, most quickly in the case of stones and stony irons, soft discolorations and rustlike blemishes.

Specialized scientific work proceeds routinely in the laboratories, Henderson told me, of which at least two examples will be of interest to the layman. The first has to do with an old cosmological problem. Radio-active dating confirms the fact that the earth and the meteorites are the same age, having existed for probably something over 4.5 billion years. Since the meteorites are relatively pure samples of the aboriginal matter, scientists hope to get from study of them vital clues about how the solar system was formed. The second concerns a new problem. Cosmic rays, high-energy bolts that flash through space, are potentially dangerous to living matter. Lesions discovered in the brains of animals exposed to extended space flights may have been caused by them. The rays also alter inorganic matter. Fresh falls are therefore carefully examined for internal molecular changes that might have been caused by this agent, thus possibly throwing some light on the rays' power to harm astronauts in their travels.

The cutting and polishing facilities are in a large room in the museum basement, where we went next. Winches with great chains for lifting heavy specimens, cumbrous and delicate cutting and grinding equipment, abrasives and polishes were there. It all

seemed much like a coarse diamond cleaving operation, handled by a short, squat museum employee
whose powerful fingers looked like cows' horns.

Above this workshop, on the first floor of the museum back of the Constitution Avenue entrance, there is
a large interior room where some of the biggest meteorites found in the United States are on display, along
with photographs, diagrams of the sites of finds,
slices of meteorites showing their structure, and other
meteoritic material. One of the photographs is an en-
largement of the first meteorite to be found on the
moon. This arrived at the Smithsonian in 1970 amid a
heterogenous batch of lunar material sent from the
National Aeronautics and Space Administration headquarters in Houston, one of the dozen of such collections
sent out at that time by NASA to various scientific
groups, for general examination. The meteorite is a
lensoid particle of nickel-iron about the size of a grape
seed. Henderson with great happiness identified it.

3

Central Park Squirrels

The squirrels of Central Park are probably one of nature's most pampered forms of free-living wildlife to be found anywhere. A while back these sybaritic creatures were the subject of an intensive if rather unconventional study by one of the nation's most eminent mammalogists. He is Dr. Richard G. Van Gelder, presently the department chairman and curator of mammals at the American Museum of Natural History whose quarters are in the building that faces the Park along Central Park West between Seventy-seventh and Eighty-first Streets. The study started in 1957, a year after Van Gelder, at the age of twenty-

41

seven, had come to the Museum as assistant curator of mammals. Each morning and evening during the project's many months he left his apartment near the Museum for walks in the Park with his Doberman Pinscher bitch, Roulette. They entered the Park at the opening at Central Park West and Eighty-first Street, usually walked south along the West Drive or over the terrain to the west of it, and exited through the portal at Central Park West and Seventy-seventh Street. While Roulette padded along at the end of her leash, Van Gelder, to the considerable mystification of passersby, frequently paused to observe his research subjects, often taking notes, sometimes while gazing aloft into a tree. The section he studied, which is west of the West Drive between Eighty-first and Seventy-seventh Streets, amounts to about 1 percent of the 690 acres of the 840-acre park that are in the form of land. Van Gelder estimated its squirrel population to be thirty animals. Were this density to be extrapolated to the Park as a whole, a population of 3,000 squirrels would result. "Obviously this would be inordinately high," Van Gelder told me recently. "The explanation is that most of the thirty were to be found clustered around the two entrances. In Central Park, entrances are locations that have a distinct squirrel survival value. The animals get most of their food from human handouts. Thus they are directly dependent on the volume of human traffic. Obviously this is heaviest around the entrances. On rainy or snowy days in particular, people will come there to feed the squirrels, but will not think of venturing into the interior. At such times the middle of the Park is virtually barren of human beings. So the heavy squirrel population about the entrances is a survival technique, and in no way indicative of the squirrel population in the Park generally."

Soon after this conversation, in an effort to get some overall idea of the number of squirrels in the entire Park, I decided to take a census of them myself. I found Van Gelder's generalization about entrances invariably to be true with the exception of the Park's northern sector. There, despite the presence of seemingly magnificent habitat for squirrels in the lordly woods crowning the Great Hill, there was a marked dearth of them, not only there but around the entrances as well. I laid this scarcity to the relatively unprosperous adjacent neighborhoods. The inhabitants, I assumed, had other things on their minds, and other uses for their money, than feeding squirrels. At the end of my census, I estimated the Park's squirrel population at more than 400 animals. Considering that considerably less than half of the Park is wooded or, for that matter, furnished even with the occasional trees that a squirrel needs for peace of mind, the population is abnormally high. Whatever the precise total, it is, in Van Gelder's opinion, at least two or three times what it would be without the operation of a neverending free lunch by visitors.

Van Gelder's study ceased in 1959, three years after it began. Three factors were responsible. His campaign of distributing mimeographed maps to fellow dogwalkers for help in the project in other sections of the park was fruitless. In the main, those he approached were extremely cool to combining squirrel enumeration with pet exercise periods. Also Van Gelder sought a scientific control for his enterprise. He wanted to squirt with a water pistol the tails, backs, foreparts, or hindquarters of different squirrels with dyes of various colors. This would allow for later identification and exact information on the range, habits, position in the dominance hierarchy and sundry other matters in connection with the animals marked. A special Parks Department license would doubtless have been necessary for the operation. From what Van Gelder could learn of Robert Moses, then the city parks commissioner, approval for such a license was highly unlikely. Finally, at this time Van Gelder was appointed chairman of the museum's department of mammals, and his workload increased.

However, the study did produce certain results other than the observation that squirrels are abundant around the entrances. The principal ones concern the almost complete urbanization of the animals. Slavishly and shamelessly, they have adapted themselves to the ways of the city. Their forebears were native stock that roamed the site's prepark woodlands 125 years ago. Squirrels in the wild are notoriously wary as any hunter can testify. Today's squirrels in Central Park, on the other hand, have lost all trace of wariness. With the four-foot-long form of Roulette straining at the end of her leash, Van Gelder has had one crouch practically nose-to-nose with her waiting for the tidbit it expected to be thrown. Squirrels who provide for themselves in the woods prefer the nut of the shagbark hickory above all others. Van Gelder, however, discovered that when it and various other nuts were placed in a line before Park squirrels habitually they simply grabbed what was closest to them. Nor do they confine themselves to a diet of nuts. They consume, apparently quite happily, Cracker Jack, popcorn, tortilla chips, Fritos, peanut-butter crackers, and even griddle cakes, to name some of the provender on their bill of fare. But, above all else, their main food seems to be shell peanuts. Visitors purchase bags of these from vendors in or near the Park and scatter them profusely for the squirrels, a practice, by the way, that may be nutritionally bad for the recipients. Van Gelder hazards a guess that the relatively large amount of fur loss and eye trouble he found in Park squirrels may be due to an overabundant diet of peanuts. Other scientists, talking of the same problems in other park squirrels, have voiced a similar suspicion.

Further evidence of the marked influence exerted by the city on Park squirrels is their flouting of the peak periods of normal squirrel activity. Characteristically, these are a few hours after dawn and the last few hours of full daylight. The Park squirrels, by contrast, are active throughout the day. I have seen a pair of them climb head downward into a Park wire waste basket to retrieve some sandwich scraps from a discarded lunch bag at the noon hour, a time when, one scientist has said, "a noontime gray is a rare and maybe an unhealthy bird." The emphatic agility of those I saw mocked any infirmity, however.

Nor do they make their own dens or nests if they can crowd brazenly into a man-made house, of which a number were placed in trees in the 1940s by Park attendants. Van Gelder once stood below a house near Eighty-first Street and Central Park West and coaxed out of it with a clucking food call a staggering total of sixteen squirrels who circled in a stream expectantly down the bole of the tree. In addition, they have turned the nooks and crannies of buildings beside the Park into shelters. I have seen several nonchalantly using the space between the sill and the old-fashioned air conditioners jutting from the windows of the museum as a refuge during a pelting rain. Also, they are traffic-wise, fearing, with good reason, the automobile, which in the Park is a main squirrel predator. Rarely do they venture incautiously onto the motor highways. The band leader Meyer Davis is on record that he saw one on the grass by the West Drive at Seventy-seventh

Noontime activity by Park squirrels.

Street patiently waiting for the traffic light to turn red before crossing the drive. Finally the city seems to have diminished their birthrate, as it has that of many of its human residents. Van Gelder noted relatively few midsummer young born after the squirrels' normal second breeding period in June, a situation that mirrors the control of offspring practiced by many of the small families housed in apartments bordering the Park.

Squirrels, found widely in the Old and New World, constitute the family Sciuridae. The species in Central Park is the eastern gray, whose range covers the entire eastern United States. The scientific name is *Sciurus carolinensis* as the species was first described from the Carolinas. The word "squirrel" itself comes from the Old French noun *esquireul*, created from the diminutive of the Vulgar Latin *scurius*, a distortion of formal Latin's *sciurus*. That, in turn, derived from the earlier Greek term *skiourous* (formed of the roots *skia*, shade, and *oura*, tail), the translation of which is "he who sits in the shadow of his tail."

The description, bestowed more than 2,000 years ago, especially fits the eastern gray. Of all the quadrupeds inhabiting eastern North America, none has a tail so splendid, dramatic, and useful. The nine-inch plume is roughly half the body length of the adult, a measurement that varies from seventeen inches in the southern part of the range to twenty in the northerly. Much time is spent fluffing and grooming it, an indication of its importance, the owner being particularly careful to comb out all bits of foreign matter. One of the unhappiest squirrels I ever saw was sitting on a low limb of a tree near Summit Rock, the Park's highest point just in from Central Park West at Eighty-third Street, trying with claws and teeth to remove some chewing gum that had become embedded in its tail.

The eastern gray depends on its tail for many vital functions. It serves as a sunshade, a blanket in cold or stormy weather, a foil and a shield in the fierce fights that often develop between males in the mating season, an expressive aid to communication, a counterbalance to effect marvelously quick turns, an aquatic rudder on the rare occasions the animal takes to the water, an aerial rudder on its customary leaps from branch to branch, and, lastly, as a parachute to soften the impact of occasional falls.

On sunlit summer noons it arches the tail over the

head like a parasol; in the dead of winter, when squirrels do not hibernate (except briefly when the temperature drops so low that it threatens life, a situation which does not occur in Central Park), the tail is wrapped around the curled-up form in the nest like a comforter, preserving body heat. Males can be seen flicking it at their foes in mating skirmishes that interrupt their pursuit of females over the bare limbs of the park trees in late February or early March; sometimes, if the skirmish becomes a battle, the tail may be brought directly into the path of an oncoming bite.

Squirrels are highly vocal, their sounds ranging from soft, friendly buzzes or purrs through barking quacks to feet-stamping, teeth-chattering rages, all invariably accompanied by ripplings of the tail, the tempo of which indicates the depth of emotion being expressed. Squirrels are not especially rapid on the ground. Leaping (the propulsion coming from the strong hind legs) is their method of locomotion there. Normal hops are twelve inches. These increase to twenty-four inches when travelling, and to a yard at ordinary high speed. Under forced draught, five feet can be covered. The top straightway speed by this method is twelve miles an hour, as has been determined by pursuing them down an enclosure with an automobile. Many creatures, including small, squirrel-chasing boys, are, of course, swifter. But the squirrel does not depend on speed for safety on the ground. Instead quick dodges and lightninglike turns, accomplished by the use of the tail as a counterweight, are its safeguards. In my observation, no small boy in Central Park, no matter how persistent, has come even close to catching one. The same is true for other potential predators, or nuisances, such as unleashed dogs. While squirrels normally avoid the water, they sometimes do, for reasons yet unclear, take to it. Forty years ago thousands swam the Hudson River from east to west north of the city, twisting their tails when they wanted to change direction in the water.

Habitually, of course, squirrels in trees leap from branch to branch and from tree to tree. Six feet is the widest level leap they have been seen to make, a distance achieved in part through the agency of the tail, which streams out behind like a glider's wing giving lift in the air and acting, as well, as a rudder to provide the desired direction. Longer leaps of twenty feet from tree to tree have been observed, but in these cases the landing point is always well below the take-off, the tail again assisting in guidance and in the glide.

Throughout the winter squirrels forage actively and, since life in Central Park is less rigorous than in the woodlands, Park squirrels generally enjoy an easier time in cold weather than their country cousins. However, they both share the dangers of an ice storm when the branches of trees are glazed with frozen rain. These so-called silver storms make for perilous footing along the limbs and after one in Central Park I have seen squirrels fall to the ground while trying to make progress aloft. The tail during the fall swings rapidly from side to side, gripping the air and acting somewhat like a parachute, and without exception in my experience the obviously embarrassed squirrel after hitting the ground picks himself up and makes off, apparently none the worse for the mishap.

This function of the tail undoubtedly was at work in what is perhaps the longest nonlethal squirrel drop on record. It occurred July 19, 1934. That morning Mr. and Mrs. Clyde Cooper of Memphis, Tennessee, after an all-night drive checked into the Hotel Lincoln here for a rest. The room clerk noted that they were accompanied by a pet squirrel, which they said they were taking south to their son Billy. In their room on the seventeenth floor, the party retired, the couple to bed and the squirrel to a towel placed for it on a chair. Not long after, the office crew on the third floor heard a thud in the nearby airshaft. At the bottom of this they found a stunned squirrel that had either fallen or jumped from an open window in the Coopers' quarters. Picking it up, they summoned a veterinarian who, while noting that the squirrel had suffered a slight nosebleed, predicted that shortly it would be all right. By four o'clock that afternoon the pet was frolicking about the Coopers' room.

Although the urbanized Park squirrels clearly prefer to reside in man-made houses, these are now in short supply. Their peak of a dozen or more was reached in the 1940s. At that time a lady refugee from Nazi Germany, apparently endowed with scant knowledge of natural history, held the unshakable opinion that the Park squirrels suffered cruelly in cold or stormy weather and should be supplied with enlarged versions of snug wooden birdhouses in which to keep warm. She demanded these lodgings of Park authorities on pain of exposing them in letters to the newspapers as heartless animal abusers. Her particular target was the late Cornelius O'Shea, the Park horticulturist, who died in 1973, an amiable person. His workmen regularly ascended trees for pruning and other duties, but soon, under feminist pressure, they were also placing squirrel houses among the branches. The lady refugee long ago returned to Germany, and only a few of the structures she demanded still remain—the rest having succumbed to the ravages of time and weather and the lack of a forceful squirrel house spokesman. A couple still persist in the Ramble, a heavily wooded area just east of the Museum, where once they were fairly common. Also among the missing is the house in Van Gelder's sector near Eighty-first Street and Central Park West. Yet people continue to keep an eye on those that are left. A lady inquired recently of the horticulturist's office about one that was missing from a beech near the statue of Jagiello, the ancient Polish King, which stands in the middle of the Park east of Belvedere Lake. When the house reappeared following rehabilitation, she telephoned her appreciation to those responsible.

With only a limited number of ready-made accommodations still existing in the Park, the squirrels do what they have always done—find or create their own. They hole up in tree hollows, which they can enlarge with their incisors, and they build nests, technically called drays, of branches, leafy twigs, and shredded bark. These last can be seen in trees all over the Park.

Drays are of two kinds, the relatively permanent, year-round nest and the more loosely built, summer variety. Both are usually twenty to fifty feet above the ground and have tops that shed water. The more permanent one is built close to the trunk and, like the other, has an entrance at the side and resembles a large ball of leaves a couple of feet in diameter. Within the nest is a cozy cavity sixteen inches across, a foot high, and lined with loose bark or other soft material. A good example of this sort of nest sits about thirty-five feet from the ground in the crotch of a red oak tree some yards in from Fifth Avenue at the level of Sixty-seventh Street. During my census walk I watched a squirrel scamper up to it bearing a bit of cloth that presumably it was going to put in the cavity. It carried the cloth by tucking it against the chest and lowering its chin.

In this sort of nest (or in tree dens or houses) during late March or April, after a gestation period of forty-four days, the female gives birth and suckles the young, which in the Park are usually fewer in number than the average woodlands litter of four or five. The newcomers are helpless and embryonic—tiny, naked, blind, without visible ears, and with limbs that are little more than stumps. Growth is slow. But the mother, equal to the male in size and strength, is affectionate and capable. She strokes and nurses the pups. In two or three weeks their lower incisors erupt, followed a week later by the upper ones. These are the animal's most formidable teeth, very sharp and strong, about half an inch long in adults. People who hand-feed squirrels in the Park should be warned not to hold the nut too tight. In an effort to get it, the squirrel may inflict a nasty bite. These teeth, too, are the ones that can cause great damage should a squirrel blunder (usually down a chimney flue) into an unoccupied house and attempt to gnaw its way out. After four or five weeks, the pups' eyes open, the triangular ears start to take shape, and the molars begin to push through the gums. These in the adult have crowns with low cusps adapted for crushing nuts, seeds, roots, and other vegetable matter. At six or eight weeks the young can take solid food as well as milk. They then begin cautiously to emerge and, staying very close to the nest, may eat tree flowers, buds, or young leaves. In a fortnight more they are half grown and fully furred and scamper around the bole of the home tree. In circling a tree, a squirrel uses all four legs separately instead of the front and back in pairs, as it does when it hops on the ground. The young usually stay with the mother for a year, after which they part company. Full growth, when they stand five and a half inches at the shoulder, is achieved at two years, but mating may start at one. The longevity of a healthy (and lucky) squirrel in the wild may, it is judged, run up to twelve years, but pet squirrels have lived several years longer than that.

The summer dray in contrast to the more permanent nest is a loosely built structure, placed well out on an upper limb. From below it may look like an untidy crow's nest. In the Park those more than one year old are usually in states of increasing disintegration. Ordinarily, they are used for only one season. The occupant almost invariably is a male. After mating, the male leads a bachelor's life with no family cares whatsoever. It employs the nest merely for lazing and resting, often curling up there with a copy of *Playboy*.

Squirrel feeders were very much in evidence on the several mornings and afternoons that I walked through the Park on my squirrel census. Peanuts far and away were the main food offered. Quantities were broadcast on the grass to scurrying beneficiaries; other feeders hand-fed individuals. Both categories of recipients often carried off the nuts for burying. The feeders themselves were a varied lot, male and female, both noncommunicative and garrulous. The most expansive of the latter was a stout well-dressed man standing on the lawn by Driprock Arch near the middle of the southern part of the Park. He was disposing of three bags of peanuts, whose contents he strewed on the turf around him to the great excitement of a throng of guests. "These squirrels," he said with obvious satisfaction, "are the best fed in the world."

Thousands of peanuts and a few other nuts are unquestionably buried each year in the Park by squirrels. Many, if not all, are retrieved during later foraging, not through memory but the sense of smell, which operates, aided by a little digging, even after snowfalls. No cracked nuts (which would spoil) are ever buried. Usually the squirrel eats these on the spot as well as, ordinarily, the first two or three offered it before it starts to bury. The burying act itself is a ritual. A longtime observer of park squirrels, the late naturalist Ernest Thompson Seton, reported on it as follows: "His procedure is always the same. He receives the nut in his teeth, then takes it in both paws, puts it back in his mouth, turns it around, licks it with his tongue, then goes off a few bounds and, with his forepaws, digs a hole in some open place, making it about three inches deep. Holding the nut in his teeth, he rams it down point first into the hole; with his snout he roots the earth back into place, tamps it down a little with his paws and his snout, replaces the leaves, combs up the grass with both paws, and goes off. If another squirrel comes along at once, the first drives him off."

Squirrels are not the only potential thieves repelled. Seton stated that a judge in a Harrisburg, Pennsylvania, park, while investigating a newly buried nut, had the squirrel rush at him and knock his hand away. After fifteen minutes, however, there was no such reaction. The squirrel seemed to have forgotten the nut, or its sense of ownership had dimmed.

Seton has also related that he watched park squirrels bury ten out of thirteen peanuts within an hour, each in a separate hole. They kept doing this under his observation every fine morning during the three months of the fall nut season, and he calculated that each eastern gray probably buried several thousand, perhaps as many as 10,000, nuts during that time.

Seton was one of the scientists who suspect that a heavy diet of peanuts is bad for a squirrel's health. Perhaps this is the reason that squirrel fur is not at its most beautiful in the Park, although here and there individuals may exhibit extremely handsome pelts. However, even the most attractive American gray squirrel skins are not used by furriers to make coats and other articles of apparel. The material for these comes from European Russia and Siberia whose climates produce tougher skins. Occasionally, a black squirrel will be seen in the Park. This is a melanistic phase of the eastern gray, very common the farther one goes north in the range, and, actually, a fairly frequent sight in parks in the Bronx. Albino eastern grays are also known, but there is no record of one from Central Park. However, at Olney, Illinois, in the southern part of the state, a colony of several hundred exists.

Squirrel health in the park, which may be teetering from a weighty diet of peanuts, is undoubtedly helped by some of the natural foods it is also known to take. In the spring these include staminate flowers of oak, elm, and maple, and the buds and young leaves of these and other kinds of trees. In eating buds, the squirrel grasps a stem with the claws of its forepaws and clips it off with its sharp incisors. Then it revolves the cluster slowly, eating the buds one by one. The claws on a squirrel's feet are not retractable like a cat's but it can raise them to keep them from being dulled, a helpful skill when moving about the pavements of the Park. After stripping the stem, it drops it to the ground. On spring bird walks through the Park I have passed trees under which the ground was heavily littered with these cuttings. Another food that squirrels like is sweet maple sap. They gnaw stems and twigs in the spring to encourage the flow and then lick the sap. If, after a chilly night, it has become frozen, they eat the sugary icicles. In the fall, of course, they are also eat acorns from the Park oaks. Water is another thing that the squirrels need once or twice a day and the Park in various places has a generous supply of it. Squirrels seek it wherever it is handy, including the zoo's beaver pool, from whose brim they can sometimes be seen drinking under the quiet, liquid gaze of the immersed owners.

At the turn of the century the Park was much wilder than at present, despite the fact that it had been open to the public for more than forty years. Contributing to this situation were fewer visitors, who also were more considerate of the terrain than today's larger crowds. Then the remoter parts of the Park, with its fairly large area of more than one square mile, had little-frequented nooks and crannies. Wandering into one, a pedestrian might almost have felt arrival in a realm far beyond the city. Witness a large, tree-shaded rock (since removed to make an entrance for automobiles at 106th Street and Central Park West) about which, at this earlier time, the late famed herpetologist Raymond L. Ditmars wrote that in its crevices were established hibernating dens for scores of brown and garter snakes which, when not in slumber, roamed the Park. Another factor was the absence of the automobile. Trees and all other living things thrived better, lacking its fumes.

The squirrels in this period, aided by excellent forest conditions and the handouts of visitors, thrived to such an extent that a thinning of their ranks became necessary. For a week during 1901 the estimated population of nearly 1,000 was reduced by 300 through the agency of attendants, who shot them. The task with the relatively tame squirrels was easy, quite a different job than bringing down those in the wild, which is one of the more difficult feats in hunting. This is because the squirrel, if it cannot reach the safety of a hollow, flattens itself on top of a lofty branch until it seems barely more than a wisp of gray lichen. Andrew Jackson supposedly won the battle of New Orleans through the marksmanship of his frontier riflemen trained on hunting squirrels in their dense native forests. (Jackson's men hunted squirrels for the pot, the meat of squirrels, which is tasty, being an essential ingredient in a now almost forgotten delicacy, Brunswick stew.)

Predators of Park squirrels in those days included some traditional ones such as certain hawks and owls, now, of course, no longer a threat. Today the greatest danger may be the automobile. Of it the squirrel is very wary. Van Gelder thinks also that feral dogs and cats, both of which are presently to be found in the Park, may prey, or seek to prey, on squirrels. Sight is the sense that squirrels use to warn of enemies. They do not, for self-protection, employ the sense of smell as do some other notable game animals such as deer.

A thing that puzzled Van Gelder quite a bit during the days of his study was the number of squirrels in Theodore Roosevelt Park, a four-block area separated from Central Park by Central Park West. This smaller park, which lies between Seventy-seventh and Eighty-first Streets and is bounded on the west by Columbus Avenue, contains the American Museum of Natural History, a few acres of greensward, and some trees whose branches contained several squirrel nests. But at times the squirrel population in the park was greatly in excess of what the nests could carry. Van Gelder strongly suspected a two-way flow of transients from Central Park. He never could prove it, however, until one morning when he arrived at the Museum very early after a light snowfall. Scores of squirrel paw prints dotted the white covering of Central Park West on which traffic was still sparse. "The squirrels were crossing both ways between the two parks, apparently just after dawn before the traffic started," Van Gelder told me.

Another plat of greenery adjoining Central Park— this one on Fifth Avenue—is also visited by similar migrants. It is the sizable garden at East Ninetieth Street, belonging to the former Andrew Carnegie mansion, now occupied by the Arts and Design Department of the Cooper Hewitt Museum. There I spoke with Manuel Perez, a caretaker at the place for forty years, the first twelve under Carnegie's only child Margaret, who was Mrs. Roswell-Miller. The garden has turf, flower beds, several large trees, and furniture where persons may sit outside, all surrounded by a high ornamental iron fence backed by stout wire mesh. "We have always had Central Park squirrels coming in and out," Perez said. "They climb right up and down the fence with no trouble at all. They are very smart. Because they come mostly when they see people outside who may give them nuts. They take the nuts and run up our trees with them."

Squirrels have, however, gone farther afield than merely to plots adjoining the Park. In what is the longest confirmed trip to date, a squirrel crossed Fifth Avenue at Sixtieth Street in early June, 1930, and proceeded to pay an extended visit to the East Side. It progressed along Sixtieth Street to Madison and Park Avenues by way of the pavement, street, trees, and house balconies, producing in the process a rash of telephone calls from residents announcing its presence to authorities at the zoo. They eventually sent a keeper in pursuit who, despite his best efforts, was unable to retrieve the agile rover. By the next day it had worked its way to Fifty-ninth Street and Lexington Avenue, now the throbbing heart of Dry Dock Country, where its appearance as it scampered gaily over store awnings, soon collected a large crowd, including many Bloomingdale's shoppers. The assemblage was shortly augmented by a solitary policeman, soon thereafter increased to four. Armed with heavy paper sacks, the patrolmen over the period of an active half hour resolutely hounded their quarry to the cheers of the gathering. Finally, after a neat bit of police encirclement, the squirrel was bagged by one Officer Mendotity who carried it unceremoniously back to the park.

Whether this is actually the longest squirrel journey that has occurred out of the Park is not entirely clear. Van Gelder always wondered during his study whether there was some squirrel traffic between Central Park and other parks fairly close to it, such as Morningside and Riverside Parks, during postdawn periods or at other times. There is some evidence that this might be the case. One afternoon Van Gelder followed along West Eighty-first Street a squirrel that crossed Columbus Avenue. It was halfway to Amsterdam when he lost sight of it among sidewalk pedestrians. "By paths that may have been known to it and in its own time," Van Gelder said, "it may have made its way to Riverside Park, which lies beyond Broadway and West End Avenue. I would say that whether Central Park squirrels can reach these other parks is still an open question."

4

Champion Tree

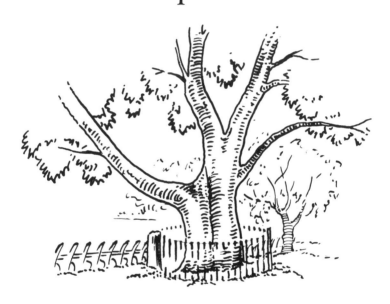

A few yards in from Fifth Avenue, back of the Seventy-second Street entrance to Central Park, stands a venerable tree, protected from public vandalism by a sturdy, square iron fence. It is a Chinese elm (*Ulmus parvifolia*), a native of Asia, planted years ago, as were so many other species of foreign trees, in an effort to make the Park something of an international botanical garden. Every spring, because the small leaves are late in appearing, the Park horticulturists may get phone calls from residents in the nearby apartment houses, fearful that the tree is ailing. But each year, as they have for decades, the leaves eventually emerge.

I happened to pass the elm a couple of years ago in the company of a botanically knowledgeable friend. He told me the tree is perhaps the oldest Chinese elm in the United States. Looking at the trunk and gauging it to be about four feet in diameter at the thickest part, I added that it was probably the largest, as well.

"Very possibly," my companion said. "Were it a native tree, or one that the American Forestry Association considers naturalized, we would know for sure. Every year the association puts out *The Social Register of Big Trees*, a list that gives the champions, in terms of size, of every native or naturalized species in the country. As a matter of fact, New York State has two champions, one of them an ailanthus tree."

Since the ailanthus is an extremely common New York City tree, I determined to round up some details about that particular champion and to learn, if I could, something about the *Register* itself.

Accordingly, I journeyed not long thereafter to Washington, D.C., where the American Forestry Association has its headquarters, and was told in the office that the *Register* began, in a preliminary way, back in 1940. My informant, Mrs. Carol S. Ronka, a pretty blonde in her twenties, who was then assistant to the Chief Forester, went on: "As you probably know, the American Forestry Association is the oldest national forest conservation outfit in the United States. It was started in 1875, and from the beginning it received occasional queries about whether such and such a tree was the country's largest. By 1940 these queries had reached such proportions that my predecessor in the job, Miss Dorothy Dixon, was delegated officially by the

Association to start a search to locate—and thus to help in the preservation of—the largest trees of each native and naturalized species to be found growing in the United States. The news media and other interested parties such as horticultural and garden societies were notified, and we were off."

The first list, published in 1944, contained champions in 228 of the nation's 865 native and naturalized species—the trees, in other words, that are said to grow wild in this country. The formal name of the list, *The Social Register of Big Trees,* undoubtedly reflects Miss Dixon's femininity. The latest, published this year, showed 581 champions, of which forty-five had ousted old rulers and fourteen were species new to the list. Fittingly enough, Florida, leading the states in the number of tree species, also led in the number of tree champions with eighty-nine. Michigan was second with fifty-six, and Texas next with fifty-one. Only ten states lacked even a single champion.

As it happened, I was present at the crowning of a new one, a black ash from the Middle West. I asked Mrs. Ronka how many of the letters on her desk might be concerned with *The Social Register of Big Trees.* "Probably several," she said. "The contest is now widely known in the proper circles, and competition among state forestry organizations and individual tree lovers gets brisker and brisker all the time." She picked up the top piece of mail on her desk and opened it. "Ah," she said. "Here's one. Quite interesting!"

The writer was Miss Dale Digrys, of Akron, Ohio. Her candidate, in the town of Bath in that state, stood ninety feet tall, was fifteen feet, three inches around the trunk at four and a half feet from the ground, and had a spread of sixty feet. Monarchs are installed by way of a point scale that concerns these three factors.

The scale reduces the trunk circumference to inches. To this is added the height, and then one-quarter of the tree's spread, these figures being in feet. According to this reckoning, Miss Digry's aspirant, compiled a score of 285 points, displacing a 235-point incumbent from Wayne County in the same state, which had ruled only since 1965. Often, these contentious days, reigns are even shorter, Mrs. Ronka told me.

New York's newer champion is a bigtooth aspen in the upstate town of Walker, not far from Rochester. It took its place at the head of its class in 1963. Bigtooth aspens, in reality poplars, grow in dry soils and burnt-over areas in southeastern Canada and northeastern United States. Usually one is under sixty feet in height, but the specimen at Walker is almost one hundred. In June, 1966, there occurred in the tree's vicinity the largest migration ever recorded on this continent of the black-capped chickadee, a number of which were observed resting in the champion's capacious branches. Aspen is also the favorite food of beavers, an animal now increasing in the state, to the delight of trappers, who often bait their snares with a tasty two-foot branch of the tree.

The ailanthus, the state's senior champion, whose reign has lasted over two decades, is of a species known by sight to practically every resident of New York City. It is sometimes called the tree of heaven, but O. Henry who was not distinguished for his nature writing, referred to it merely as the "backyard tree." A native of China, it has been here almost 200 years. The bark is gray and coarse, and its rather crooked branches carry exotic-looking compound leaves. These, late to come and late to go, have a somewhat tropical appearance, especially when dancing in a breeze. Comparatively thick leaf stalks measure from a foot and a half to a yard long, and carry eleven to forty-one leaflets, which are of a brilliant green no matter what the weather. In June, the trees, separately sexed, like the willows and certain others, produce inconspicuous, yellowish-green flowers. Wind and insects do the pollinating, and by late summer large, crowded clusters of samaras, or key fruits, hang heavy on the female trees. The seed, so light that 17,000 of them are needed to make a pound, is a small black dot at the center of a pair of twisted wings—a much more efficient flying machine than, for example, the single-bladed maple key. Partly because of this device, the tree grows not only in Brooklyn, where it was celebrated in a novel some years back, but uniformly throughout the five boroughs, in backyards and in outright waste places where other trees would fail. It thrives in cracks between bricks. Cockily, it pushes tufts of green through iron gratings of apartment-house areaways, rising from what appear to be beds of sheer concrete. A poet once remarked that in this city two dead vine leaves, a cigarette butt, and a paper clip provide ideal growing conditions for an ailanthus. He hardly exaggerated. A fifteen-foot specimen was found flourishing a few years back on a corner of a garage roof in the lower Bronx, sustaining itself handily on dust and roofing cinders. Winds take the light seed surprisingly high, and the tree's characteristic branches can often be spotted drooping over masonry facades in terrace gardens 100 feet up. The ailanthus exceeds all our other trees in speed of growth. Young ailanthus trees often add eight feet in height a year. Once established, they are almost indestructible. Suckers sprout twelve feet tall in one growing season from the stumps of felled trees. A botanist has predicted that when Manhattan falls in ruins it will soon be covered by ailanthus. A start has, in fact, been made in that direction. According to Parks Department records, there are 2 million trees, including a few elderly ailanthus, in our parks, and half a million, including virtually *no* ailanthus, line our streets. But the department estimates that elsewhere, despite its policy of uprooting young ones within its jurisdiction and granting no permits for street plantings, half a million ailanthus of various sizes are now growing enthusiastically among us, far more than any other species.

Pollution from industry and from the automobile has long since done in many of the old-fashioned American trees that used to embellish our city streets. Plane trees and other modern replacements often turn sickly, as well. Sulphur dioxide, carbon monoxide, and gobs of soot are currently the three main pollutants of our air. The ailanthus somehow resists these. All trees feed themselves—and thus start the preservation of their health—in exactly the same fashion. The first requirement is water. To put it most simply, just back of the bark, inside the thin growing layer called the cambium, lies the outer wood, the sapwood, and this contains tubes that carry up water obtained from the earth by the roots. The tubes grow thinner and thinner, until, through the thinnest of all, the water passes into the leaves. Every molecule of water in a tree, it has recently been discovered, is bound to others like links in an extremely strong chain, so that as the leaves use up the water more mounts by means of the liquid linkage —often 100 feet or more. Of course, trees must breathe air as well as drink water. On the underside of each leaf are tiny holes, opened and closed by guard cells, which admit air. Using water, carbon dioxide from the air, and the energy from a bit of light, the leaf, with the aid of its chlorophyll, produces sugar and pure oxygen. The oxygen it returns to the atmosphere through the leaf holes, and the sugar, which is the raw food of all tree species, it keeps. The sugar descends by way of cells on the outside of the thin cambium layer to whatever part of the tree requires it. Trees ordinarily languish or die under urban pollution, either from the clogging of the leaf holes, which produces a form of strangulation, or from the presence of too large an amount of noxious gases in the air that the leaves take in, which produces a form of toxicity, or from some combination of the two. Under these conditions, certain trees buckle completely. Others perform marginally, at best. The ailanthus seems unaffected. In fact, it can prosper where pollution is worst. Botanists do not yet know the secret of its elastic metabolism. One of them said recently, with a sigh, "If the ailanthus were suddenly to become a tree of prime commercial importance, we would have a good chance of learning the key to its pollution resistance. Scores of researchers with scads of money would zero in on it. Alas, this doesn't seem likely to happen. The tree is widely regarded as a weed."

The national champion, which no one could conceivably regard as a weed, is to be found on the North Shore of Long Island, thirty-five miles from the city's eastern boundary, at Sherrewogue, the estate of Francis M. Bacon III, who is a stockbroker (Harvard '21), and Mrs. Bacon, who is Toni Frissell, a photographer whose work has often appeared in *Life* and *Vogue*. The Bacons usually spend the first four days of the week in the city and then go to the country for a three-day weekend. Having asked and received permission to call on them at Sherrewogue, I drove out there one summer weekend several years ago to see the tree, accompanied by its nominator for the championship, George H.

Peters, of Climax, New York. A past president of the Long Island Horticultural Society and a onetime deputy commissioner of public works in charge of Nassau County parks, Peters retired some years back to a home in the Catskills, but he and Mrs. Peters then had an apartment in Freeport, and I picked him up there in the middle of the morning. A trim, blue-eyed man of seventy, he looked and acted twenty years younger, as is often the case, I find, with those who spend their lives close to plants.

We entered the Bacons' place by a road running through extensive, well-planted grounds. After a hundred yards or so, we stopped, at his suggestion, and got out to look around. Stony Brook Bay, a sizable sheet of water, lay to our left. Beyond it to the west was the peninsula of Nissequogue. Perhaps another hundred yards ahead of us stood the Bacons' house. It was an imposing three-story wooden structure, painted white, and in front of it, and partly concealing it, was the champion. "There!" Peters said, with animation. "You'd never think *that* was a cussed-out, despised, and generally maligned form of plant life, would you? Twenty years ago, when I first heard there was a big ailanthus on the Bacon property, I came over all full of excitement, but I wasn't prepared for a giant like this."

And giant it was—a fountain of green, shooting up nearly 100 feet, with a wide trunk and a vast spread of branches. Peters continued to gaze at it fondly. Then he told me some of the details of its discovery and coronation. "I first heard of it from Mrs. Herbert G. Meserve, a holly breeder over there in Nissequogue. She owns an estate with the unusual name of Holly-by-Golly. Back in 1947, egged on by the publicity surrounding the publication of the American Forestry Association's first *Social Register of Big Trees*, we in our horti-

The champion ailanthus tree.

cultural society decided to list the notable trees we had on Long Island. I was put in charge of the project, and we fanned out all over. Five years later, in 1952, the survey resulted in the publication of a booklet called 'The Trees of Long Island.' I nominated this ailanthus that year as national champion, and it was accepted. Its statistics then were: height, eighty feet; spread, seventy-five feet; and trunk circumference, eighteen feet, eight inches. It displaced an ailanthus in Queen Annes County, Maryland, whose trunk circumference was almost a foot smaller and spread ten feet less."

I asked Peters if he knew how old the tree was. "I would judge it at something over a century in age, and to have been planted here as a young tree a decade or so before the Civil War," he said. "That was the era when wealthy men from the city were buying estates along the North Shore and beautifying them with all sorts of native and exotic flora. It became the habit, too, with people who already had places here. Notice that larch over there, and that copper beech, and especially that weeping beech. All are desirable ornamentals. The weeping beech, like all others of its kind in the world, is the descendant of a deformed sapling that long ago sprouted in the garden of Baron DeMar, a Belgian nobleman, who ordered it destroyed. Instead, his gardener cared for it and developed it into the graceful thing that botany now calls the weeping beech. In 1847, Samuel B. Parsons, a nurseryman of Flushing—which was then, and had been for some time, a center of nurseries in this country—was touring Europe in search of rare plants. He bought a shoot of the weeping beech and brought it in a flowerpot back to Flushing. There it grew into what a famous British horticulturist has called the finest tree of its kind in the world. The tree now stands on Thirty-seventh Avenue and Parsons Boulevard in Flushing, and the city has bought the land around it and made a park for its protection. This one here is also a beautiful weeping beech. As for the ailanthus, its position in a prominent place before the house and its size, which indicates an age of over 100 years, both point to its having been part of the estate-beautification program that went on around here about that time."

We got back into the car and drove on toward the tree. It stood some sixty feet in front of the house, amid a sizable planting of boxwood, off to one side of a loop formed in the driveway for convenience in turning. On the other side of the loop was a pond, with mallards floating on it. The part of the tree's massive trunk that faced the house was covered with a shroud of English ivy.

"Let's see what the trunk measures now," said Peters. Carefully parting the box, which, in the sunshine, exuded its characteristic dusty-spicy smell, we reached the trunk, and Peters took from his pocket a twenty-five foot steel tape encased in a leather-covered reel. He put one end against the gray, creased bark and asked me to hold it, which I did. Then he circled the bole, passing the tape over the ivy at the required height of four and a half feet. "Nineteen feet, nine inches," he said. "Make it nineteen eight, allowing for the ivy."

We both backed out of the box, and Peters stood for some moments looking up at the champion. "Not much growth in the last ten years," he said. "It's grown only about three inches in girth this past decade, as against nine for the previous. Age is making itself felt. And it's lost some leaders, too." He pointed toward two cuts sawed flush to the trunk and covered with preservative, where limbs had once grown ten or fifteen feet above ground. "But the cuts are solid," he went on. "So the tree continues healthy." Many ailanthus at maturity, which for the average tree is forty to fifty years, fall victim to heart rot. Then the interior of the trunk and larger branches grow hollow, and the tree's life expectancy is short.

Just then, a caretaker passed by, and Peters asked him how the limbs had been lost. "In an ice storm a couple of winters ago," the caretaker said.

"There's one of the weaknesses of the ailanthus," Peters told me. "Ice storms and high winds frequently damage it. Because of the fast rate of growth, the wood is rather weak, you see. Yet what nature takes away with one hand it gives back with the other. Ailanthus, for example, is notably resistant to both insects and diseases. It even weathers salt water. Along the seashore, high, hurricane-driven tides don't kill it when they pass over its roots, whereas they do virtually all other trees."

Between the champion and the house I noticed a smaller ailanthus, and I asked Peters about it. "The big tree is a male," he said, "and that is an offshoot. It rose from the large tree's root, and is, of course, also a male. The ailanthus reproduces itself not only by seed but also by this method, which is called suckering."

It was now almost noon, and we walked up to the front door, where we were greeted by the Bacons, who had invited us to join them for lunch. "We'll eat in today," Mrs. Bacon said, "although often in the warm weather we lunch in the shade of our tree. I love looking up at its elephant-hide bark. Some years, mallards build a nest in the lowest crotch. The hatchlings tumble to the ground with no harm done, and make a beeline for the pond, where they grow up—if the turtles will let them. We've had this place for thirty-odd years, and the family before us, the Devereaux Emmetts, had it for fifty-some. Early in their ownership, an iron standard that held a lamp to light the roadway was fastened to the tree. Now the trunk has engulfed it, and perhaps the lamp as well."

I was surprised to hear Mrs. Bacon say that the house, which is quite large, dated back to 1689, since early-Colonial dwellings were usually far less imposing. "Oh, originally this was just a two-story farmhouse," she said. "Stanford White designed the west wing, and somebody, sometime, added a third floor and other considerable trimmings." The village of Head of the Harbor is in the township of Smithtown, and Mrs. Bacon told us that the whole area had been sold in 1663 by Lion Gardiner's widow to Richard Smith, Jr., a former soldier of Oliver Cromwell who trained a bull as his riding animal and was known far and wide as Bullrider Smith. A statue of the bull stands a few miles to the west of Sherrewogue, where Routes 25 and 25A intersect. The Bacons' house was originally built for Smith's second son. Smith's own place was across Stony Brook Bay, on the peninsula of Nissequogue, on part of what is now Holly-by-Golly. Mrs. Emmett, from whom the Bacons bought Sherrewogue, was born a Smith. The Indian name, long attached to the place, means "across the water" in the language of the Montauk tribe.

Ailanthus talk dominated lunch. It seems that the first ailanthus known to have entered this country arrived in 1784. William Hamilton, of Philadelphia, a grandson of the man who designed Independence Hall, planted it as an ornamental in his garden. (This garden, called the Woodlands, is now a part of Woodlands Cemetery, adjacent to the campus of the Uni-

versity of Pennsylvania, in downtown Philadelphia.)
But the ailanthus didn't really become well known
hereabouts until after William Prince, another Flushing nurseryman, brought it to Long Island, in 1820. His
nursery, one of the nation's first, had been started in
1732. It was so famous that when the British took over
Flushing during the Revolutionary War, General Howe
appointed a guard to save it from harm. By 1840, partly
through the efforts of Prince, a persuasive salesman,
the ailanthus was common around New York. Streets
were lined with it. Linden and horse chestnuts (which
had bugs) were displaced to make way for it. City
burghers drove their elegantly cushioned carriages and
barouches under it. Their country cousins, in what
are now the outskirts of the city, burned it for fuel,
ranking the wood with oak, black walnut, and birch
for a clean, hot flame.

Then the tide turned. Ailanthus on the Capitol
grounds in Washington, D. C., were rooted out. Citizens
began attacking the tree in the public print. The reason was the male's flowers. These briefly each spring
give off an unpleasant odor. "Disagreeable" is one description, "putrid" is another, and some critics point
out that the carrion fly, among other insects, aids in
pollination of the species. I asked Mrs. Bacon what her
response was to the smell of their tree. She replied
that for the first week or ten days in June a sweet,
sickly fragrance hovers around the champion, which
could certainly be called disagreeable. "As it's grown
older, though, this is less noticeable," she said. The pol-
len itself is not in the class with that of beech, birch,
elm, oak, and poplar. These cause almost all tree-oc-
casioned allergies. A couple of people in Brooklyn
Heights, however, are known to suffer from ailanthus.

The scientific name, meaning "tallest heaven

tree," is *Ailanthus altissima*. How the species acquired
it is a tangled story of the sort that is common among
plants. Before Linnaeus, botanical nomenclature was
chaotic. No system existed for telling precisely what
plant was being talked about. After his introduction, in
1753, of standardized description, based on the use of
one word to describe the genus followed by one word
to describe the species, the confusion lessened. Since
then, the first botanist to publish a definitive description of a plant has chosen the name. But, as the final
authority, the International Botanical Congress maintains a nomenclature committee to resolve problems.
Ailanthus, the generic name, was given in Paris at the
end of the eighteenth century by René Louiche Desfontaines, a distinguished botanist. He had seen the tree
growing there in the garden of the first physician in
ordinary to the king. Unfortunately, he also saw a picture of what he thought was the same tree in a book by
a pre-Linnaean scientist concerning the flora of the
Molucca Islands. The native name was *ailanto*, or tree
of heaven, from the lofty height. Desfontaines Latin-
ized this to *ailanthus* and added the specific name
glandulosa, for the two small glands each leaflet bears
at its base. The ailanthus had arrived in Europe only
shortly before this—in 1751, when Father d'Incarnaville, a French Jesuit living in Peking, sent to the Royal
Society of London some seeds of what he thought was
the Nanking varnish tree, a commercial plant of high
value. Evidence exists that he knew the winged seed
of the ailanthus, but the seeds he sent had somehow
lost their wings, and Father d'Incarnaville did not recognize them. They grew, however, producing not varnish trees but ailanthus. One planter, an Englishman
named Miller, describing it seventeen years later as
a new plant, placed it in an already established genus.

He called it *Toxicodendron altissima,* or tallest poison tree, on the ground that being around it in the greenhouse gave him headaches. Thus, the tree entered botanical literature with two names. Early in this century, the nomenclature committee set about straightening things out. In 1906, it approved *Ailanthus glandulosa*; then, ten years later, a scholar noted that although Miller had erred on the genus, his species name had preceded Desfontaines'. Accordingly, the committee gave *altissima* preference over *glandulosa*, and the name is now presumably set forever.

Although the first specimen of the ailanthus we see today arrived in America in 1784, paleobotanists have examined petrified relics from Montana that show the ailanthus, looking very much as it does now, was present on this continent more than 60 million years ago. *Eohippus,* the dawn horse, scampered under it. Climatic changes wiped it out on this side of the world, but in unglaciated parts of Asia it survived, along with a form of insect life that lives on the tree as an apparently harmless parasite. This is a large, beautiful moth, tan with reddish markings, called *Samia cynthia.* Although the moth's caterpillars feed on the ailanthus leaves and attach their cocoons to them, tree and insect seem to thrive in each other's company. In China, the cocoon's rough silk is spun into stout pongeelike cloth, so strong that a nineteenth-century American scientist wrote that garments made of it lasted through several generations of wearers. This information caused many efforts a hundred years or so ago to establish in this country a silk industry based on the ailanthus moth, but none was successful. I asked the Bacons whether they had ever noticed any evidence of the moth around the champion. Mrs. Bacon said she had seen big green caterpillars, about three and a half inches long, near it. These were the full-grown larvae. Entomologists in search of the cocoons find them readily in Central Park and on Convent Avenue and 141st Street, under the ailanthus that stands before the old Alexander Hamilton mansion.

Ailanthus altissima now grows in many parts of North America. But it dislikes frequent subzero temperatures, and ventures only as far north as Massachusetts, from there ranging west to Iowa and southwest to Texas. It is the most northerly of about a dozen ailanthus species, most of the rest of which are tropical and native to southern Asia and the Pacific islands. *Ailanthus altissma* favors the Temperate Zone in Asia as well as in this country, and extends as far north as Peking, where it is common as a street ornamental.

Mr. Bacon said he thought the pond near the tree had helped the well-being of his own large specimen.

"Doubtless true," said Peters. "Water is very important to a tree, producing heft and health. The average ailanthus dies before sixty years of age. Yours is twice that, and seemingly hale."

Mr. Bacon said he wondered how long the champion might last.

"It's hard to say," Peters said. "There are signs that its life mechanism has begun to slow down. But it could easily last another thirty-five years."

"I hope it's here as long as we are," Mr. Bacon said.

After lunch, I dropped Peters at his Freeport apartment and drove back to midtown Manhattan by the Belt Parkway, the Brooklyn-Battery Tunnel, and the East River Drive. Almost everywhere, except in the tunnel, I passed ailanthus fronds stirring in the light breeze. Botanical reference books list many uses of the tree around the world. Its plantings check erosion in dune areas of the Black Sea. Afforestation is its contribution on the bare slopes of the Alps, timber in New Zealand. In China, an infusion of the powdered bark, yellowish-green and of strong, nauseating odor and bitter taste, is prescribed as a cure for tapeworm and dysentery. Here, of course, the tree's only function is to refresh those who look out of rear windows or up from tables in backyard cafes at its verdant flounces. They are green, always green, even in the hottest summer, and, in a domain of bleak masonry walls, they lift the heart.

5

City Conservation Officer

Some years back, when Anthony Mazza bore the official title of New York State Game Warden of Manhattan, he used to receive indignant telephone calls almost daily concerning a modish lady accustomed to walking a deer at the end of a leash over the paths in Central Park. Mazza, who earlier had investigated the situation, knew that the deer was a fallow deer, a native of England, and thus its owner was not in violation of state conservation laws through harboring a protected animal, a fact he patiently imparted to his callers. Eventually Mazza, who has a good deal of the diplomat in him, persuaded the lady her pet would be happier in a zoo, and the calls ceased.

Mazza, after performing this and other peculiar chores during the space of a third of a century, expects to retire when his department can find a satisfactory replacement to take over his duties which can truthfully be called rather singular, although the search admittedly may take quite a while. Knowing this was the case, I sought him out not long ago for several talks about a career that has not many parallels in this country. At the time of our meetings, he was a burly widower sixty-six years of age, actually still several years removed from compulsory retirement, since this step is mandatory for a conservation officer only after he reaches age seventy. Mazza has a square, kindly face set in a six-foot frame that easily carries 215 pounds. Nineteen forty-one was the year that the New York State Department of Conservation appointed him Game Warden of Manhattan, certainly a strange-sounding title for a man laboring in the concrete precincts of Manhattan. Yet that was his official moniker for half a decade, a phrase that very inadequately hid an odd variety of duties for the officer who, from time to time, referred deprecatingly to himself as "just a game warden to skyscrapers." Five years later, the borough of the Bronx was added to his territory, thereby increasing responsibilities that the average citizen may never have known existed.

Mazza is the senior among five officers doing conservation work in the city, and the only one to handle two jurisdictions. Brooklyn and Queens each had one when I saw him, and there were two for the relatively open spaces of Staten Island. Often Mazza worked with them and with nearby suburban colleagues, part

of over 200 officers that the state maintains to enforce its fish and game laws in territory where such
enforcement might normally be expected. Sometimes,
too, Mazza told me, he was assigned to those areas, as
was the case early one spring when he journeyed north
to Ogdensburg, a town on the Saint Lawrence River.
Walleyed pike by the thousands were entering a stream
that flowed through the town to spawn in its shallow
reaches. It was weeks before the legal season opened,
and residents were taking the fish by nets and snatch
hooks. "Poaching was childishly easy," said Mazza,
who is generally known as Tony. "The pike, some of
them three feet long, were lying quietly in the water
like so many logs." Mazza with a force of brother officers soon stopped the infractions.

His mates upcountry, working in forests and along
trout streams, never derided Mazza for his largely
paved domain. Instead, they knew the extent of his
job, and were respectful. "Deer jackers, checks for fishing licenses . . . undersized bass, that sort of thing—
our task's simple," one of them told Mazza as he was
departing Ogdensburg. "But not yours. You've got responsibility. You have to know just about the whole
conservation law—shellfish, lobsters, live-animal import-
ing, furs, license enforcement, gun rules, plumage,
commercial fishing, and the legality of game and wild-
fowl prepared for restaurant kitchens."

The statement was no exaggeration. New York
City, particularly Manhattan, is a lucrative market for
those dealing in virtually every fish and animal covered
by the state conservation law. This ordinance, embrac-
ing more than 700 printed pages, is very broad, sufficiently so, in fact, to daunt some conservation officers.
But Mazza is just the person to love a broad statute.
Before he was ten, his father began regularly to take

him out of the city, where he was born, on hunting and fishing trips, a procedure that lasted for many years, during which the young boy acquired insight into the breadth and complexity of ecology. The strong early impressions gained in woods and by watercourses never left him. So drawn was he, in fact, to wild things that in 1939, at a time when he had risen to assistant superintendent with a building construction company, he took the state game warden examination, passed it, and accepted the Manhattan position as soon as it opened two years later. "I probably could have made a lot more money had I stayed in the construction business," Mazza said, "but I've never regretted the decision I made, not for one moment."

Not long after he left the construction company, he found himself again atop a building, this one a completed structure, the Hotel Pierre, across from the southeast corner of Central Park. A pair of duck hawks had nested on a cornice, and were feeding pieces of pigeons to two half-grown chicks, behavior that brought complaints from passersby and hotel tenants, who watched feathers drifting slowly earthward into the street. Hanging head down over a parapet, his legs clutched by two porters, Mazza was able to elude the parent birds' swoops and remove the young. He carried them across Fifth Avenue to an acquaintance, a bird keeper at the Central Park Zoo who had a way with nestlings. When they were fledged, Mazza took them across the Hudson River and released them above the rocky slopes of the Palisades, which is great country for hawks. The parents, meanwhile, checked out of the Pierre once the young were gone.

Mazza covers the sixty-four square miles of his two jurisdictions (more than twenty-two on the island of Manhattan and more than forty-one in the borough of the Bronx) in a brown, four-doored Ambassador sedan of recent vintage, equipped with a two-way radio but carrying no distinguishing marks on its exterior or license plates. In the course of his duties, day or night, Mazza drives rapidly and expertly over the two boroughs' 1,300 miles of streets that he knows far better than the average taxi driver. Above the car's radio, taped to a sun shade, is a copy of the Official Ten Signal List of the Associated Public Safety Communications Officers, a lengthy schedule running from 10-0 to 10-99, and including such calls as 10-32 (Emergency) and 10-57 (Hit and Run). Mazza's responsibilities also include the coastal waters of the two boroughs. These comprise twelve square miles for Manhattan and twenty-seven for the Bronx. To monitor them, Mazza uses one of the department's fleet of two dozen motorboats that are berthed in the metropolitan area, the largest of which are three thirty-two foot craft, the remainder being smaller various-sized outboards.

On assignments out of the city Mazza wears the conservation officer's uniform, an outfit much like that of a state trooper with campaign hat, Sam Browne belt, a leather holster with revolver, and in a narrow pants pocket a short billy. The revolver has played a relatively unimportant part in Mazza's thirty-three year career. "But there have been times," he said, "when its presence has given me considerable comfort." He also carries a worn two-sided folding leather wallet, one face of which bears a card with his photograph, his name and a summary of his duties, the other holds his badge, a small silver-colored shield three inches high emblazoned with the arms of New York State and the number 169.

In town he wears ordinary business clothes and usually dispenses, as well, with the revolver and billy except on those assignments where he thinks one or both might be useful. Such an occasion, as a matter of fact, came not long ago, when he called for a red fox at the Manhattan headquarters of the American Society for the Prevention of Cruelty to Animals. He arrived with the billy in a coat pocket. The fox had been picked up on the street some days earlier, trailing a leash. "The owner did not call for it," said Mazza. "Apparently he knew that a fox is an illegal pet, being a protected species in the state." The animal was put in a cardboard carrying case and placed on the floor in the back of Mazza's car. The pair started in mid-morning for the Bronx Zoo, which had agreed to take the vagrant. Halfway there the fox, without Mazza's knowledge, gnawed its way out of the container. Mazza first became aware of this when, from under the front seat near the heel of his foot that was resting on the gas pedal, the fox's head appeared, making ominous noises. The situation, in the midst of characteristically heavy New York City daytime traffic, demanded quick action. Mazza tapped the fox smartly on the head with the billy. Twenty minutes later the animal revived in the clinic of the zoo veterinarian, apparently none the worse for the experience. Shortly thereafter it was put on exhibition.

Mazza's customary urban attire of ordinary business clothes permits him to make the kind of arrest in the city that he accomplished a few years back. He was put on the trail by a welcome tip. Besides his own patrolling, Mazza's work is greatly aided by tips—or complaints—that he gets from radically conservation-minded members of the public and also from radically competition-minded business competitors. This tip, from the latter group, led to the West Washington Market, a large wholesale meat mart in downtown Manhattan that often carries sizable supplies of game. To be sold legally in such a place, deer, for example, must have on the carcass's four quarters and the two ears state tags, costing five cents each, showing the animals were killed legally to thin out a herd or were raised in captivity. In the market Mazza spotted two white-tailed deer carcasses bare of such markers. Possession of such meat is not a violation of the law. Sale of it is, however. Mazza with his inconspicuous clothing and kindly face, which could have belonged to any meat-hungry New Yorker, had no trouble in purchasing the deer. He then promptly arrested the dealer, who was fined $300. Not long afterward, the four market hunters from New Jersey who supplied the meat were also arrested and fined. As is the practice with such seizures, the food was sent to a charitable institution.

A conservation officer's police powers are quite extensive. Mazza, naturally, needs a search warrant to enter a home. But whenever a conservation officer has cause to believe the environmental conservation law is being violated, he requires none to look through the trunk of an automobile or a public place of business. Also, he may use any necessary force during such examination and search. Furthermore, possession of any contraband is presumptive evidence of guilt upon which the possessor can be held. A summary arrest can be made any time the officer witnesses a violation of the conservation law or any other law.

Mazza, however, uses his authority sparingly. In the case of an individual first offender, he usually invokes the mildest of his three alternatives. This is called a judgment by stipulation. In it, the offender, having admitted his guilt, is taken before Mazza's superior, Captain George Thilberg, who has quasi-judicial power to settle cases out of court. This method, however, is by discretion of the department and only in the interest of expediting certain types of arrests. It is not a general practice in all cases. Thilberg, in charge of the department's law-enforcement unit in Regions 1 and 2, which comprise the metropolitan area, has his headquarters in Stony Brook, Long Island. There, a civil settlement having been agreed upon by Mazza, Thilberg, and the offender, the latter is permitted to pay the settlement, is given a warning about further transgressions, and dismissed without acquiring a criminal record. The settlement is in accordance with the schedule and penalties set forth in the law. The law also provides for an additional sum for each illicit item, which could run as high as $25 for each fish, bird, or lobster illegally taken. Reporting for this type of transaction is the same as a court compromise with abstract transmitted to the comptroller. Copies of such abstracts are on record in the regional office for consideration in repeat violations in which case the penalties would be greater and most probably referred for a court disposition. Mazza told me he liked to handle first offenders via the compromise route because, he said, "It seems to me right to think of what is best for conservation. A first offender warned, and given some educational talk by the arresting officer, is a better risk, it seems to me, for the future of conservation than a first offender made angry and rebellious by being stung with a heavy penalty plus the record of a court conviction. Of course, in instances of premeditated wrongdoing like the West Washington Market case, the stipulation, or compromise, is not used."

Most other arrests are for violations handled by criminal process, and many are withdrawn to allow civil compromise, which does not carry the stigma of a criminal court record. Misdemeanors, however, involve a criminal court record on conviction. In the city Mazza would take the offender straightaway to the closest police precinct station house from where the violator is transferred as quickly as possible, usually the same day, to the nearest appropriate court, generally a magistrates' or Special Sessions tribunal for adjudication. On rural-area assignments, Mazza brings the apprehended party promptly before the nearest justice of the peace. An example of a criminal case would relate to the illegal taking of deer. Infringement of the deer laws are looked upon very seriously by the department.

Mazza's arrests run, he said, "in spasms." Some years there were only a handful, in others forty or more. He spends, as a rule, little time in court, generally clearing the case the same day. His arrests all plead guilty. "I never made an arrest unless I had clear evidence," he said. "Where there was doubt, I gave a stern warning." Fines, imprisonment, or both may be ordered by the judge, depending on the violation by the offender. For certain misdemeanors, fines may range to $1,500 and/or imprisonment to one year.

Corporate cases differ. These are handled initially by lawyers for the department and those of the firm under indictment. Sometimes they go to trial, sometimes they are settled by negotiation out of court. In the spring of 1973 Mazza joined forces with his Queens associate and found more than 100 cartons of alligator watchbands in the factory of one of the largest watchband dealers in the country. After March 30, 1971, the sale or possession for sale, of articles made of alligator hide had become illegal in the state unless the company had invoices showing prior arrival of the goods. The company had no such invoices. Two dozen watchbands were taken by Mazza and his colleague for evidence and turned over to department attorneys for action in the case which at the time of going to press was still in legal channels.

The previous November, working with two nearby suburban officers, Mazza and the others discovered at a fur company's office in New Rochelle thirty-one articles of wearing apparel, mostly coats and jackets, made from the skins of spotted cats—leopard, ocelot, and jaguar—and also ten tanned leopard and jaguar skins. These items were as illegal as the alligator watchbands without prior invoices. Again the company lacked them. That case, too, is still in the hands of the department's lawyers.

The law apparently violated in both these corporate cases concerns trafficking in endangered species of wildlife. The animals involved, besides those mentioned, whose names appear in Part 182, entitled "Traffic in Endangered Species of Fish and Wildlife" of the state conservation law, are 390 species of domestic and foreign mammals, birds, reptiles and amphibians, fish and one foreign mollusk, *Papustyla pulcherrina*. This last is a brilliantly colored green tree snail about an inch long, which is disappearing from its habitat rather too rapidly to suit conservationists. The snail is restricted to Manus, a 600-square-mile island of the Admiralty Archipelago, lying in Melanesia in the far western Pacific Ocean. Lumbering of the trees on which it lives and a brisk worldwide demand by collectors for its shell are causing its decline.

Mazza during his more than three decades of service saw some notable changes in the department. One was when his original designation as game warden became, a few years back, that of conservation officer and another, in 1970 was when it was lengthened to environmental conservation officer. This last came at the time when the formal title of the department itself was expanded to that of the New York State Department of Environmental Conservation. The character of his work by then, too, had become somewhat altered. An instance of this involved the many pet shops in town. Generally speaking, they no longer required the close monitoring that they once did when, for example, in the 1950s and 1960s they often attempted illegally to sell dozens of foreign goldfinches. These birds were in heavy demand by the city's canary owners, who number 25,000, according to a local authority, Mrs. Virginia Belmont, of the Belmont Bird and Kennel Shop in Rockefeller Center. "Now the pet shops—like the public in general, I suppose you could say—have become more conservation-minded and tend to follow the law precisely," Mazza said.

One aspect of his job, the part he dislikes most, has not changed, however. This is the confiscation of wild creatures that are children's or family pets. Many households, returning from a summer in the country, bring back with them animal foundlings—squirrels, foxes, possums, birds of prey, songbirds, and so on, all of which are protected species. The retention of them by private parties is against the law. They have usually been found when in a young, helpless state, nursed to health by their rescuers, and later taken by them to town to lead a city life. Mazza with his strong feelings for nature appreciates the affection that can exist between pet and family. But by law he has no choice. Once apprised of such a situation, he has to go to the address and take the animal away. His latest visit, a few months before I saw him, was to a house on the upper East Side. A youth of fourteen there had kept a raccoon in the backyard for two years. The raccoon would climb affectionately all over the boy, sometimes perching contentedly on his shoulders like a tame monkey as he walked. The confrontation, as usual, depressed Mazza enormously. But in the end his sympathetic diplomacy produced an answer satisfactory all around. He did not appropriate the animal at once. Instead, he talked at length with all members of the family, asking them to consider overnight the advantage to their pet of living with others of its kind at the Children's Zoo in the Bronx, which had earlier agreed to take it, rather than a lonesome, unnatural life away from its kith and kin. Mazza also pointed out the pleasure it would give other persons to see it there, not to mention the family's own pleasure when its members would arrive to visit it. The next day Mazza drove up to the zoo accompanied by the pet and its owner who said he now felt fine about the solution. Birds or animals that zoos, in or out of our city, wouldn't take Mazza releases in suburban woods.

During the course of our meetings I spent part of a day accompanying Mazza on his rounds. We met by appointment at 6 A.M. at the corner of Fulton and South streets in the middle of the Fulton Fish Market, the largest fish market on the country's East Coast. On Mazza's advice, I wore rubbers to guard against the icy slush and water on the stall floors. Four blocks away, my taxi driver complained about the smell. Following our greeting, Mazza told me that sometimes the odor clings to one's clothes long after leaving the place. We were at the heart of a busy, hectic scene extending over the market's six blocks—wet concrete floors, open overhead lights, wooden stalls, hand trucks pushed by yelling men whose usual language was obscenity. Several greeted Mazza in that fashion. He looked at me and smiled. "When they call you 'sir' down here, you're in

trouble," he said. Almost at once a little man sidled up
to Mazza and whispered in his ear. He was a tipster reporting that earlier that morning a business rival had
gotten in and had sold some undersized striped bass.
Since the fish were gone, Mazza said, "I'll check him
tomorrow." Across South Street under a shed in another part of the market two young couples clad in
evening clothes strolled along. The men bore opened
beer bottles in their hands, and the foursome seemed
to be putting an end to a long evening by visiting what
is certainly one of the city's more unusual sights. Mazza
remarked them, too, and smiled again.

"Yes, this is an unusual spectacle, the hub of the
piscatorial wheel," he said. "A fish market that started
in 1821 now with customers as far west as dealers in
Chicago. Work starts here at one or two in the morning
with trucks unloading supplies from the fishing ports,
and ends about 9 A.M." A kaleidoscope of seafood was
visible during my walk—shrimp, shellfish, squids, and
octopuses; huge tuna and cod, some as long as a man;
rounded butterfish like little silver platters; mackerel
with lustrous blue-black lines threading their backs,
making their close-packed ranks, seen from above, resemble abstract, vermiculite patterns; even small sharks
a few feet long purchased, Mazza said, by the Harlem
and Chinatown trade.

At Wallace, Keeny Lynch Corporation, dealers in
lobsters, Mazza asked an employee to open one of the
stacks of live lobster crates from Maine, containers
which were held together by wire fasteners. Mazza then
removed a small silver-colored metal gauge from his
pocket. It was roughly oblong with two prongs at one
side that were three and three-sixteenths inches apart.
These were for measuring the lobsters to see if they
were the legal length. In the middle of the gauge was

an opening one inch wide and one and a half inches long. Selecting three of the smallest lobsters in the crate, Mazza measured them. A lobster is legal size in this state if it runs at least three and three-sixteenths inches from the base of the eye socket in front to the back end of the carapace, the horny shield that covers the body before the tail sections start. Mazza put the gauge on them, and all three lobsters conformed to standard. At a nearby stall, Mazza measured some clams. Quahogs, often called cherrystones, are legal size if they are at least one inch thick and thus fail to drop through the hole in the gauge. Steamers, on the other hand, are legal if they are at least an inch and a half long and stay on top of the long portion of the hole in the gauge. The clams inspected also all passed muster.

We then moved to a stall loaded with ice-packed, opened boxes of striped bass. Their size caught Mazza's eye. He greeted the dealer by name, then said, "They look kind of small. Where did they come from—Amagansett? I thought so." He took a retractable metal tape from his pocket and, addressing me, said, "Stripers are the only fish measured from the nose to the *fork* of the tail. They must be sixteen inches that way. Other fish are measured to the *end* of the tail." All three fish he selected and measured were barely legal. "Tell your supplier to watch it," he said to the dealer. "These are getting awfully, awfully close." Mazza told me that stripers of the same age, and therefore approximately the same size, swim together in schools. "That's the rule—from shorts, as we call them, to cow bass like those over there," he said, pointing to some enormous stripers of more than fifty pounds, lying on a counter. "When the bass are running just a mite short, there is some temptation to try and get by with them. That's why I spoke to the dealer. As to why cow bass are called cow bass, I couldn't tell you unless it seems that they're as big as a cow."

We rambled on through the market with Mazza performing various checks but finding no illegalities. Each stop was brief until we came to a stall on the west side of South Street, where some bearded, black-hatted rabbis were studiously examining species of freshwater fish—carp, mullet and whitefish. That, too, required little time, but in the stall next to it, Mazza hailed an old acquaintance, a Board of Health man, who was clad in a long white coat like that of a medical technician and wore a brown paper bag upside down on his head as a hat. There, some conversation for my benefit ensued. The technician was doing one of the periodic tests that the department makes at the market, taking samples of shellfish for a coliform count to see that they do not come from polluted waters. Coliform bacteria are always present in sewage. In the samples of clams and mussels that the Board man was taking, the bacteria count to be found in the later tests would have to be at, or below, the allowable level, or the Board would prohibit sale of more from those waters until the situation cleared up. Because of pollution, shellfishing is prohibited in all waters off the shores of the city. The ban does not apply, however, to most other forms of fishing.

We next stopped at a stall on Fulton Street where Mazza usually rests for a moment on his visits. We had barely sat down when in walked a tall, broad-shouldered, open-faced girl carrying easily in her hands a heavy burlap sack full of mussels. She asked the proprietor who was standing nearby if he would be interested in being supplied with mussels like these, a virtually unlimited supply of which were in waters near her home in New Jersey, she said. This talk brought Mazza to his feet instantly. He inquired if she had a license to sell mussels. She did not. For a moment it looked like the young lady was in hot water. However, the proprietor confirmed that she had phoned him the previous day asking if she could show her mussels. And she gave to Mazza the correct name of the official to whom she had applied for the proper papers as a vendor. As a consequence, Mazza became convinced that she had brought her mussels in only as samples to show to the stall's proprietor and to those of several others in the market to whom she had telephoned. He thereupon canceled his intention to confiscate the mussels and arrest her. Later he said, "She was straightforward, and I believed her. Furthermore, I admired her gumption in finding this kind of work for herself. I also admired the way she hefted that sack of mussels."

We left the market about eight o'clock in Mazza's car. I put my rubbers in a tote bag that I had carried and placed it in the back of the automobile. We stopped at a diner in the financial district for breakfast, Mazza first using the two-way radio to call his office in Stony Brook to give his whereabouts and his next stop. That was 12 Monroe Street, an apartment-house complex a few blocks north of the fish market. Mazza was looking for one R. Santo who had been apprehended some weeks before by a conservation officer on Shinnecock Bay in eastern Long Island with a catch of undersized summer flounder whose legal length is fourteen inches. The man had failed to make his court appearance, and Mazza had been asked to find him. Inquiry, however, revealed no R. Santo at that address. "False name or address, probably," said Mazza. "This happens if you don't take the violator at once to a court, which is the safest practice. Or, if the courts are closed, make him show a document bearing positive identification and address such as a driver's license. I'll get back to the arresting officer and see if he has details that may aid us in finding the man."

From Monroe Street we drove north to 325 East Third Street, the office of M. Schwartz & Son, a feather dealer and importer. On the way up, Mazza said, "Ninety percent of the country's feather business is done in this city, and Schwartz is perhaps the oldest and largest firm. Like most of the citizenry, the feather merchants now know and respect the conservation laws. One rarely finds anything amiss in their stock these days." This was far from the case when Mazza began his work. "Sometimes we'd deplume a hat with an eagle feather in a department store window. Or take the hat itself. Then we'd go to the dealer who'd sold the plumage and nail him," Mazza said.

The big battle against the ladies' millinery feather trade began around the turn of the century, and took years to win. The reason was monetary. Aigrettes, a favorite decoration, are the fifty or so long, snowy-white back feathers that form the nuptial train of the male egret, a species of heron, which was killed in order to acquire the feathers. Aigrettes brought $32 an ounce. To give some idea of their comparative value, the price of gold in 1900 was $20.67 an ounce. By the end of the First World War, largely due to legislation sponsored by the Audubon Society, the taking of plumage became illegal and the vogue for it on hats ended. However, in 1937, because of loopholes in the law, it revived. During 1941, the year that Mazza began his job, the loopholes were finally closed, again principally through efforts of the Audubon Society. Small amounts of illegal plumage continued to trickle onto the market, but in general the dealers bowed to the legislation. To show compliance, many voluntarily withdrew from their stocks all eagle, egret, bird-of-paradise, and heron feathers. Trucks, supervised by Mazza, took several loads to vacant lots in the Bronx for burning under the eyes of observers, at least one load of which was estimated to be worth $25,000.

The Schwartz premises consist of offices and a warehouse quartered in an elderly building eight stories high. Every room, including the offices, seemed crammed with cartons, huge paper sacks, burlap bags, paper barrels, and more than 5,000 coffin-sized wooden packing cases, all filled with feathers or the skins of birds. Some of the containers seemed antique enough to date back to the company's founding in 1910. We were greeted by Irwin I. Schwartz, the owner and the son of the founder, a small gentle man in his sixties, and by Irwin's son, Michael, aged twenty, who for the last year has been learning the business. Irwin Schwartz is the man who created the red-feather symbol for Community Chest drives across the country. Membership is now symbolized merely by tiny plastic feathers given to donors. But, originally, at Schwartz's suggestion, drive officials bought actual small red feathers from him to give to those who had contributed to wear in coat-lapel buttonholes or on dresses to show that they had subscribed. Schwartz also is responsible for the fad of feathers in men's hat bands. He first affected the style himself, liked it, and, in the late 1930s, persuaded the window decorator of the Truly Warner hat store at Fifth Avenue and Forty-second Street to put a few hats in the window with Schwartz feathers. Immediate public acceptance followed. It still exists to some degree today among those men who continue to wear hats.

Around us were sacks with tightly wound rolls of feathers several inches long called marabou, a booming feature of the Schwartz business just now. Marabou in the early annals of fashion was the name for the long soft tail or wing coverts of the marabou stork, a native of Africa. These, sewn together in strings, were used from 1800 on to trim ladies' dresses and negligees. Now the term has been expanded to apply to any kind of poultry feathers—turkey, chicken, or other domesticated fowl. They are cut, dyed, and sewed into strips, in Hong Kong or other areas of cheap labor, and used for the same purposes as the original marabou. A number of women were emptying the sacks and putting the feather rolls in shipping boxes to fill orders.

Mazza picked up two long feathers from an open carton nearby and said to young Michael, "Let's see how much you're learning. Which of these is the Korean and which the English pheasant feather?"

"I know that's the English," said Michael, pointing to one. He was right.

"Now," said the older Schwartz to Mazza, "let's try you."

In a moment Schwartz was back with a truly enormous feather, at least four feet long. The feathery part was a soft, purplish brown. On one side it was ornamented with black-enclosed white circles the size of silver quarters. Around these, and on the other side of the quill, black and white striggles were interwoven like the pattern of a boa constrictor's skin. It was a striking exotic plume.

"What is it?" asked Schwartz.

"An argus eye," said Mazza. He had given the correct commercial term for the tail feather of the argus male pheasant, a native of dry, rocky country in Malaysia and eastern Asia.

"For that, you can have it," said Schwartz, handing

it to Mazza. After a pause, he continued, "I have more. Can I sell for millinery?"

"No," said Mazza. "But yes for flytying." The present law permits any kind of feathers to be used by anglers for tying flies.

"Flytying," said Schwartz dejectedly. "A thousand flies to a plume. Millinery takes all." He made a face.

As the four of us wandered through the eight floors, Mazza spot-checked containers here and there. He found all in order. On one floor I noticed stacked, yellowing cardboard boxes marked with the names of songbirds. Inside were the bird heads attached to complete skins. "Alas, for the days, long ago," said the elder Schwartz, "when ladies wore birds on their hats."

"Now you can use them for flytying," Mazza joked. This time both Schwartzes made a face.

Our next stop was the "21" Club at 21 West Fifty-second Street. Periodically, Mazza investigates markets and restaurants that sell domestic and imported game and fowl. That day it was "21"'s turn. He parked by the curb, and, before locking the door, placed back of the windshield a note saying that a state conservation officer was in the restaurant on official business.

Entering by the basement door, we met Edward Quigley, the establishment's steward. At the moment, he was rather unhappy. He had just tried to order 300 Scotch grouse from a dealer and had been told that all Old World feathered game had recently been placed under a ban. Notification had come from the Department of Agriculture office in the Customs House on Bowling Green. "That means all plover, pheasant, woodcock, ptarmigan, grouse . . . you name it . . . that come from across the ocean," said Quigley morosely.

The government had found a bone disease affecting the marrow in the birds and felt it might be dangerous to human beings.

"Well, help yourself. Look around," said Quigley, after imparting this gustatory bad news, and he left us.

Mazza started for a large, glass-fronted refrigerator against a wall. "I'll tell you one thing," he said to me as we walked toward it. "I visit a lot of restaurants. If something falls on the kitchen floor here, you can pick it up and eat it, the place is that clean. You can't say that about many places." Looking around me, I saw no reason to dispute the statement.

The interior light in the refrigerator went on as Mazza opened the door. It was moist and chilly inside with plenty of space for us to stand upright. We entered. Around us, awaiting customers, were various eatables. A number were dressed pheasants, under whose wings Mazza showed me the small blue metal New York State tags, indicating legal processing. "These were probably reared on farms and dressed by the owners. They buy the tags at a nickel apiece and put them on the carcasses. It's a great time-saver for the department, believe me. Some years ago, when a big dealer like Nathan Schweitzer downtown got in a shipment of 30,000 birds, I would have to spend two or three days a month on the premises, attaching the tags by hand," Mazza told me. On another rack he showed me birds with a gold-colored tag, indicating they came from outside the state. "Quail from Wyoming," he said. Elsewhere a few untagged birds, bearing labels with names, were being held for customers who had shot them, and who would have them eventually prepared by the chef.

After spending another quarter of an hour scrutinizing the food in various compartments around the basement, we departed from an infraction-free "21" and stood for a moment beside Mazza's car. I asked him, on the occasions that he visited large wholesale refrigeration plants, how he could tell dressed venison that lacked its skin from veal or beef in a similar condition. "There are always a few hairs sticking to the carcass," he said. "Bend one. If it stays bent, it's venison; if it springs back, it's beef or veal," He went on to say that he also checks markets that make a specialty of selling unusual game. "One of these is the Maryland Market on Amsterdam Avenue," he said. "It carries such things as buffalo, hippo, wild boar, and llama, when it can get them. There's quite a sale for exotic meats in this town—aoudad steak, Mexican pronghorn antelope, and so on. Convention dinners and even private families." Once, he had to confiscate two black bear carcasses sent into a market. The animals had been legally shot in season out west but imported without proper permits. Smoked black bear hams were known to be a delicacy in pioneer days, and bear flesh, if properly butchered and prepared, has some admirers today. This continent is also the source for the black bearskins that make the tall fur hats of the British grenadier regiments, two skins to a hat. But they must be dyed first to achieve a uniform color. "During the times when market meat becomes short, one of the things I'll have to be especially careful of," said Mazza, "is venison taken by illegal market hunters showing up in markets and restaurants."

We moved out of midtown, taking our way north on the East River Drive. The fifteen miles to our next destination was covered rather quickly, I thought. Mazza has an enviable familiarity with city arteries and drove steadily just below the speed limit. Hunters Island was our goal, the most northeasterly section of the most northeasterly land in the city, which is Pelham Bay Park. The park, containing more than three square miles, is the city's second largest, only Jamaica Bay Wildlife Refuge on the city's southern boundary, composed not of a single piece of land but of water and numerous islands, ranking ahead of it. Because of Pelham Bay Park's fairly remote location, it remains in parts quite wild. We travelled across the spacious macadam parking lot that serves the users of Orchard Beach, a swimming site lying in the middle of Hunters Island's eastern shore, and proceeded into the extensive wooded northern section, following a rutted dirt track barred to ordinary traffic. Sizable trees rose all around us. A fairly thick understory of briars, bushes, and shrubs lay below them. "Raccoon, skunks, rabbits, and fox are all here," Mazza said. "So is the hybrid ring-necked pheasant, now a common game bird in the United States. If, for example, you come into these woods at six-thirty on a winter morning, as I sometimes do, you may run across fifty or seventy-five pheasant rising into the air or running through the brush during the course of ten minutes. That's a nice thing to see in the city."

"Right over there," he went on, pointing in a westerly direction, "is a lovely little spring. Water as sweet as you'd want. And here . . . have some blackberries. The price is right." He had stopped the car and within arm's length beside the open window at which I sat were berry-laden briars. I picked half a dozen of the plump ripe fruit and ate them, savoring their sunwarmed tang. We had seen no people thus far in our drive, but Mazza said there were little settlements, some of them year-round, hidden here and there in the trees, whose residents make use of the spring. Mazza sometimes gets valuable tips from these woodsy people.

We then came to a low, rather marshy spot in the road, lined on either side by a long, thick stand of phragmites, tall reeds with feathery tops, whose stems, when bitten by insects, exude a sugary substance, gathered long ago by the Indians for sweets. A boggy spot appeared ahead. Mazza turned to me. "Say a few 'Hail Mary's,' " he suggested. The car made it through, but not without difficulty. "Prayer did it," said Mazza with satisfaction. We came out near the shore of a long, narrow lagoon to the west of Hunters Island. Several fishermen were busy on both sides of the water. "In winter, after a bad northeaster," Mazza said, "I have seen this lagoon hold 50,000 duck—redheads, canvasback, greater and lesser scaup, mallard. A great shelter against the wind. Even during a storm the water can lie as flat almost as a table."

We returned to the middle of the island by another track, and farther along on it we met two city police officers patrolling on motor scooters. They were surprised to see our car. Mazza identified himself, however, and they let us proceed. We ended atop a grassy knoll to the north of Orchard Beach. The long expanse of Pelham Bay and Eastchester Bay all the way down to Throgs Neck Bridge lay before us. Here and there it was dotted with watercraft. Some of them, Mazza said, were lobstering. "This is one of my favorite lookouts," he told me.

From it, the week before, working on a tip, he had spotted a lobsterman in Eastchester Bay who he thought was responsible for selling short lobsters to a restaurant on City Island, a community that lies off the south shore of Hunters Island connected to it by a causeway.

Lobstering in Eastchester Bay.

He waited until the middle of the afternoon, the time that lobstermen bring their haul ashore, and once the catch was docked, he examined it. Years before, he had learned the perils of approaching a violator at sea. On that occasion, working in full uniform and assisting a Queens colleague in Jamaica Bay, he was after illegal netters of striped bass, since sport fishing only was legal in the bay. It was a stormy night, and the two officers were in one of the Department's large speed-boats. Its searchlight picked up the netters in a battered old craft that had, it turned out, however, surprising speed. A chase ensued over the thirty square miles of the bay, but despite the Department boat's best efforts the other kept its distance. Shouts by the officers to halt had no effect, either. Mazza could see the pursued men frantically shoveling fish overboard. At last he drew his revolver and fired a warning shot, the only time in his career he pulled the trigger on assignment. The boats were rising and falling on the choppy waves. As a consequence, the bullet, aimed high, went low and hit part of a superstructure just above the head of one of the shovelers, tearing out a chunk of wood the size of an orange. "When I saw that, I was more scared than the violator," Mazza told me. The shot brought the other boat to a halt. But by then the evidence was gone. This was not the case, however, with the lobsters on the City Island dock. A number of shorts were found and the lobsterman, an eighteen-year-old first offender, took a settlement by stipulation and paid a $200 fine. The shorts were re- turned to the water.

"This stretch between the Throgs Neck Bridge and the Connecticut boundary is as fine lobster ground as any area in the country. And I'm including Maine," Mazza said. "This fact is becoming better and better known and, with the demand heavy and lobsters selling wholesale around $3 a pound, there's lots of activity here." Lobsters are crustaceans equipped with one large claw for crushing prey and a smaller one for tear- ing it. Their food consists of fish, dead or alive, almost all invertebrate animals, and small amounts of algae and eel grass. The east North American coast from Labrador to North Carolina is their habitat. They dwell on virtually any kind of bottom—rocky, sandy, muddy, or a combination—and in water from 6 to 600 feet deep. The largest lobster brought in to date was caught about 125 miles off Long Island about ten years ago. It weighed forty-four and a half pounds. The girth of the crushing claw of a lobster this size would be twenty inches, virtually the circumference of a man's head.

Legal size is reached at from five to eight years of age, the warmer the water the quicker the growth. "Lobsters barely legal, however, are not quite old enough to breed," Mazza said. "Personally, I would like to see the limit slightly extended so that this could happen."

Just then the car radio crackled. The words were impossible for me to decipher. After a minute or two of listening, Mazza chuckled. "A lady member of Congress is with some of our officers on waters off Long Island's north coast," he said, pointing to the land that was visible across the water to the east of us. "It's the old mossbunker complaint, and she's investigating." It seems that striped-bass fishermen, a large and vocal segment of anglers, are firmly of the belief that purse netters who fish for menhaden, often called mossbunker, also take stripers. Mazza says the matter comes up year after year. The striper fishermen want the mossbunker boats barred from certain grounds. Mossbunker are small, herringlike fish, probably the most numerous fish along the East Coast. They swim near the surface and the bunker boats purse seine them, selling the catch for bait, oil, feed, and fertilizer. Also schools of stripers can be seen feeding on the menhaden. But the question is whether the stripers swim too deep to be taken by the bunker seines at the surface. "When the menhaden leave, the stripers seem to be far less plentiful," Mazza said, "and the sport fishermen think the bunker boats have netted them. Actually, it's more likely they have followed the menhaden. Bunker netters need licenses. Netting stripers would violate the conditions for granting one. They do too well, in my opinion, to risk license loss. The officers across the sound should take the lady aboard the bunker boats. Then she'd see no stripers are there."

It was now time for lunch. Mazza drove to a diner in New Rochelle just over the city line, where we ate. Then we parked for a while on the grounds of Glen Island Park, overlooking the same scene as before, but from a little farther north. "This is another one of my lookouts," said Mazza. "A clear view for miles. With the rocky shore around us, doesn't this remind you of Maine? A floating lobster pound is near here, just offshore in my area. The fisherman caches his catch there till he feels like selling. From time to time I take an outboard and check its contents, as I did a couple of weeks ago, just to be sure everything is legal-sized."

Mazza said he thought he would wait around the area until two or three o'clock that afternoon and again examine the catches of lobsters brought ashore at City Island. He asked me if I would like to accompany him. I declined, feeling his earlier description of short lobsters had given me a sufficient idea of what he might run across. Furthermore, I'd been up since five o'clock that morning. I picked up my tote bag with the rubbers, thanked Mazza, bid him good-bye, and took a taxi to the nearest subway terminal at East 233rd Street.

6

Big Rain

One afternoon during the summer of 1970 I stood in the vestibule of a town house just off Central Park West. I was hoping to snare a taxi, for outside a torrential rain was descending. When my companion and I peered toward the Park, we could see the branches of the trees sagging downward under a deluge that had turned the outdoors into a world of streaming crystal.

I said I could scarcely remember a heavier rain.

My companion, however, sniffed. He remarked that only the year before, more than twenty inches of rain had come down in several hours in his section of Virginia.

When comprehension of what he said had registered with me, I replied that the statement seemed incredible.

"Nevertheless, it's true," he answered.

Then and there I decided that I must learn what it was like to have lived through such a downpour. Within a fortnight, I had.

"Man, I'm telling you, it rained. It layered water." The speaker, a farmer with worn, weathered features like those of the lean cowboys that ride the range in the never-never land of Marlboro-country cigarette ads, was standing on the red soil of Nelson County, Virginia, and talking to me of the exceptional storm that had visited that relatively obscure part of the central section of the state the previous year. It had begun late in the evening of August 19 and had ended early in the morning of August 20, 1969. In a period of eight hours, the storm deposited upon the 471 square miles of the county—and in such quantity uniquely here in all the state—an amount of rainfall that closely approaches a world's record. According to a congressional report printed some six months after the event, a maximum amount of thirty-one inches of rain descended. The people at the National Weather Service (then the United States Weather Bureau), while citing their verified maximum of twenty-seven inches, estimate that the entire county received, in that relatively brief space of time, an average of sixteen inches—more than the state of Wyoming gets in a year. If Nelson County's remarkable rain were dumped on Manhattan, the island would be covered with almost thirty feet of water. Governmental scientists refer to the storm, with characteristic restraint, as "a meteorological anomaly," but their studies reveal that in this case the "anomaly" was something that by their own calculations could happen less than once in a thousand years.

Before I went to Nelson County I stopped at the Office of Hydrology of the Environmental Science Services Administration in the United States Weather Bureau office in Silver Spring, Maryland, to see John T. Reidel and Francis K. Schwarz, who had made a study of the Nelson County rain, and to ask them why there had been so anomalously much of it in such a relatively small spot. The rain, I learned, had been a by-product of the tag end of Hurricane Camille—a storm, well remembered in the South, that entered the country at Mississippi's Gulf Coast, along which it did tremendous damage; crossed that state and the states of Tennessee and Kentucky; and finally made its exit through Virginia into the Atlantic Ocean. In southern Mississippi, it dropped an average of eight inches of rain, and in Tennessee half that, and by the time it reached eastern Kentucky the storm seemed to be drying up. Precipitation there was between one and two inches. The two meteorologists told me that the factors commonly required for rainfall are water, particularly in the lower atmosphere, and a mechanism to precipitate it. The ordinary rainstorm, for example, develops when low-lying air containing moisture is lifted by solar heat to a point above the earth's surface at which cooling temperatures cause condensation; the moisture then falls as rain. The Nelson County storm, they said, was quite different. Although by the time Camille had crossed eastern Kentucky and entered Virginia very little moisture was left in its lower levels, and thus, in a sense, the disturbance was rained out, there remained at its center, as it moved south of Nelson County, winds with a velocity of about twenty-five miles an hour, going, as is customary, in a counterclockwise direction. For several days, there had remained stationary over eastern Virginia a large, harmless, low-lying mass of warm air whose origin was the tropical ocean. The lower levels of this were completely saturated with moisture. As Camille, whose front was then about a hundred miles wide, approached this moisture-laden air mass after dark on the evening of August 19, its winds began to draw in and pull up the warm, moisture-filled air and carry it north and northwest, until it was directly over Nelson County (and, to a lesser extent, the counties immediately adjoining it).

"Camille's winds, as in an ordinary rainstorm, took the moist, warm air high up, and then the moisture condensed and fell as rain," Schwarz told me. "But instead of the rain's gradually moving east, as weather normally does, the anomaly occurred instead. For some reason—the causes are still under study—the wind center of Camille slowed down, and the mass of wet tropical air stayed put. Thus, Camille was able to draw from it, hour after hour, the enormous amounts of water that fell on Nelson County, and it was only after several hours that the weather began its characteristic eastward move. Anomalies of this type are often accompanied by exceptionally severe electrical phenomena. Much lightning occurs, associated with sharp claps of thunder, which are due to the sudden expansion of the air in the path of the discharge." The precise details of what causes the severe electrical demonstration are still unknown, the weathermen explained, but, in general, it comes as a result of the positive charges imparted by rapid motion to the moisture particles in the air.

Riedel and Schwarz were two of three meteorologists (the third was John Miller) who prepared background material for a report on Camille made by the Office of Hydrology that was read into the record of hearings held in February of 1970 by the Special Subcommittee on Disaster Relief of the Senate's Committee on Public Works. In reference to what happened in Nelson County, the report says:

> This storm was one of nature's rare events. It is estimated that the maximum rainfall associated with this storm has a return period well in excess of 1,000 years. . . . Another measure of the rarity of this rainfall is that the maximum amount of 31 inches approaches the probable maximum rainfall which meteorologists compute to be theoretically possible during the time of rainfall involved.

Schwarz closed our talk by saying, "Much as I would like to say otherwise, an anomaly of the sort we have been discussing here has never, to my knowledge—owing to the still inexact science of meteorology—been predicted."

Nelson County is a rough square, a little better than twenty miles on a side, sloping off the eastern edge of the Blue Ridge Mountains onto the Piedmont, the high central plateau of our Middle Atlantic and Southeastern states. It has around 12,000 inhabitants, most with names and faces not unlike those of the men who fought at Trafalgar beside the British admiral whose surname it happens to bear, for Nelson County, like most of Appalachia, from Virginia to Georgia, is still as Anglo-Saxon ethnically as most of the nation was in the early nineteenth century. Nor does Nelson County move much more rapidly than it did then. At the time of the storm it had the following commercial statistics.

Three-quarters of the county—the hilliest in Virginia east of the Blue Ridge—was forested. There were no incorporated communities. Lovingston, the county seat (pop. 679) lay on U.S. Route 29, the county's primary thoroughfare, which carried heavy automobile and truck traffic from Baltimore and Washington to Lynchburg, Scottsville, and other towns outside the county. Farming was adapted to the land's hilly nature. Apples and peaches were the largest cash crops. Beef cattle were next in importance, and there was much part-time farming. Some families had worked the same land for six or more generations, since the first settlers arrived, around 1720. If the county was commercially unimportant, sparsely populated, and obscure, it nonetheless had, perhaps for these very reasons, a quiet, tranquil, outdoorsy beauty. Bear and deer inhabited the forests. Grouse were found in the hills, and the calls of quail were common.

The county has two main rivers—the Rockfish to the north and the Tye to the south, both of which feed into the James River, the county's southeastern boundary. A tributary of the Tye has the highest waterfall in the country east of the Mississippi River: Crabtree Falls, whose splendidly cascading water drops almost 2,000 feet in five segments over a distance of approximately two miles. The county's two main rivers are fed in the hilly country by numerous creeks—Hat Creek, Possum Trot, Davis, Cub, and Little Joe, to name a few.

Before I arrived, I had made an appointment by telephone with the county sheriff, William N. Whitehead, a man who, I assumed, had been in a good position to observe what had happened during those dark hours on August 19 and 20, and could direct me to remaining evidences of damage, which I wanted to see. I met Sheriff Whitehead in his office, in the basement of the county courthouse—a charming, white 1810 building set among maple trees and young glossy-leaved magnolias. Fronting it, on a stone pedestal, is a smaller than life-size Confederate rifleman. The electorate in the South seems to favor sheriffs of imposing physique, and Whitehead proved to be a good example—a gray-haired man in his middle forties, stalwart, trim in his brown uniform, and standing six feet five inches tall.

"August 19 started out pretty much like any other normal summer day down here," Sheriff Whitehead told me. "It was hot and a little bit muggy. The Charlottesville *Daily Progress*, the daily paper published nearest to us, had a weather forecast saying 'Rain likely tonight, ending tomorrow.' Right, too, on both counts. That day happened to be the day of the state Democratic runoff primary for governor and attorney general. Voting was light. The polls closed at seven in the evening, and I stayed around here till all the vote was counted. It didn't take long—an hour or so. Then I drove over home, to my house by Hat Creek—I'm about in the middle of the county—and had supper. It was a little after nine o'clock then and starting to drizzle.

"Because I was interested in the returns from the rest of the state, I turned on the television and watched it while I ate. The weather prediction on it, I remember, was 'Showers, clearing by morning.' Along about eleven o'clock, I got a call from one of my deputies, who lives in the southern part of the county—in a place called Piney River, after a stream that flows nearby. He's also one of the volunteer firemen there, and they do rescue-squad work. He said it was raining pretty hard down there, and he and some others had been pumping out basements in a few houses. In one basement, an earth wall had given way, and they'd had to run for it.

"Well, I didn't think anything of that. We'd had floods in this county before, and next morning everybody woke up all right. Little later, this same deputy calls again. Says his uncle, farther south, had called and asked to be evacuated. He had a one-story house like many in the county. It was built on a hummock, with one side facing the Piney River. The river was in flood, and the water had his house surrounded. He was like in a castle ringed with a moat, and the water rising steady. He kept calling his nephew and telling him to bring him out in the fire truck. 'That water's coming in through the house,' he said. He couldn't get out, you understand, yet he expected my man to get in. That fire truck does have pretty good clearance, so the deputy tried twice, but he couldn't make it. Low places in the roads filled with water stopped him. On the last call, with his uncle whooping and a-hollering, my man says, 'I *cain't* get to you. If that water keeps on a-coming, Uncle, you best spend the night on the roof.' He did.

"Before the last call from that deputy, another deputy calls me from down that way. 'Sheriff, the people getting crazier and crazier,' he says. 'Fellow calls me just now and says we're losing automobiles to water on Route 29'—by which he meant cars were sliding off the road into some streams. I didn't know what to think about that. We do get some crank calls. I figured this was one.

"By about one, it was really raining where I live. My wife and I had gone to bed about twelve. We sleep in a one-story part of the house that has the kind of tin roof lots of houses around here have. I stayed in bed until two and tried to sleep, but it wasn't really possible. The rain struck the roof like a giant flail being whopped onto the metal. Then, at intervals, there would come an entirely different kind of noise. Whomp! Whomp!

Whomp! It was like the roof was under a waterfall. Not single blobs of rain hitting it but like a cascade, falling in jets and spurts. Then that kind of rain would stop for a while.

"One thing that made sleeping especially difficult was that along about that time there was lightning and thunder. My wife is very frightened of electrical storms. The lightning was brilliant and almost constant, it seemed, accompanied by the sharpest claps of thunder I ever heard. But in between these there was another sound—a roaring like forty jet airplanes were stationary overhead. 'It must be that hurricane picked up speed again,' my wife said. 'It must be blowing dreadful outside.'

"Finally, at two o'clock, I got up to look out the window. The inside window was up, but we'd closed the storm window to keep the rain out. An inch of solid water was running down the pane, so I couldn't see out. I opened the window, and I got three surprises. They were so sharp they were practically shocks. First, the lightning was almost constant and very low, seeming to be practically parallel to the ground. Second, the lawn outside, which slopes down from the little swimming pool we have, was covered with a solid sheet of clear water inches deep, rushing by the house toward the creek. Third—and this was the biggest surprise of all, though all of them were pretty big, let me tell you —was that I had expected to find a screeching wind outside and it was absolutely still. Not a breath. In the lightning flashes, the tree limbs hung down, the lower ones almost touching the ground with the weight of the water, and they weren't moving at all, looking frozen in the eerie light. The roaring sound we heard was the sound of water moving over the land.

"I was struck dumb for a bit. Then we decided to

dress and wake the children. I tried to turn on the light, but we had no electricity. And although we didn't know it then, the phone was off. We put on some clothes and made our way through the house with candle and flashlight. On the second floor, I woke up my daughter, Nancy, and our two sons, Dick and John. John was in high school and the other two were home from college for the summer. 'Put on your clothes, children,' I said. 'I don't know what's going on outside.'

"Then I went out on the porch. Hat Creek, in front of our place is normally about ten feet wide and a foot deep. Now I could see it was about 200 yards wide and must have been twenty-five or thirty feet deep, with white-capped waves cresting six feet high. It was yellow. The water coming off my slope was like blue-green glass, but Hat Creek was yellow, and boulders and tree trunks and root stumps were in it, being carried along like toys in a millrace. The creek was still about seventy-five yards away from us and ten or fifteen feet below the house. In the air was the smell of freshly uncovered mountain soil mixed with water. If you ever were to take a spade and go up one of our mountains and turn out a shovelful of earth and put water in the hole, you'd get the smell at once. A characteristic, unforgettable smell, pungent and musty. So I thought to myself, There must have been slides. Somewhere some ground's come loose."

(After the rain, C. J. Koch, a soil scientist with the Department of Agriculture Soil Conservation Service in Virginia, said that soil had slid off the slopes because it could no longer absorb the storm's moisture, and that the slides were further encouraged by the fact that the season had been the wettest in a long time, the county having suffered a decade of drought. But no seasonal drought, however severe, could have prevented landslides in Nelson County that night. Koch said that in many places the soil covering the bedrock on the hillsides was about two feet deep. The pore space between the particles in that kind of earth can hold from one to one and a half inches of water per foot of depth, Koch said; that is, two feet of it can hold three inches of water. After that, the soil begins to acquire a liquid nature, and the greater the precipitation is the more liquid it gets, until it's like gruel. Then it runs off its foundation, gathering speed as it descends and carrying all before it—boulders, trees, and buildings—until it reaches a flat space or is carried away by a stream.)

Sheriff Whitehead went on: "When I thought about slides, I thought about going up the hill to see Mother, who has lived alone in the big house about a third of a mile up there since Dad died, at ninety-six, a couple of years ago. I knew that if water reached her we'd all need an ark, but slides were something else. The older boy and I got to my car and, ever so slowly, started along the road up the hill. We could still move all right because the water was running off on either side of the road. I parked in front of Mother's house with the headlights full on, and I blew the horn until she came down and unlocked the screen door. Then I went out through the rain to the porch, holding my hand at an angle over my face to keep the water out of my nose and mouth.

" 'Mother, get dressed,' I told her.

"She protested. 'Pshaw, boy, there's been rains here before.'

" 'Not like this,' I said. 'If I have to take you out of here, I don't want to take you out in your nightclothes. I'll be back if there's any need.'

"She went back in to get dressed, and meanwhile

I thought I'd drive out through the county—particularly down to the southern part, where I'd got the first bad reports. I wanted to assess the situation and see if there was anything I could do.

"It was then almost three o'clock, I'd say. My older boy asked to go with me. I said all right. We drove very carefully south on Virginia Route 151, which runs near my place, till we reached the Tye River. The bridge at that point is a solid structure thirty-five or forty feet above normal high water and about forty feet wide, with concrete sidewalls four or four and a half feet high. I got as near the bridge as I could. The lightning had subsided, but my headlight beams shone right across where the bridge was. No bridge was visible, and no concrete sidewalls were visible. All that was there was water—with cresting waves higher than those on Hat Creek. And between me and the bridge the water was eating away the bridge approach. And then, in the middle of the river I spied this telephone pole. I estimated it was twenty-five feet long. It came bobbing along, and it must have struck the upstream sidewall of the bridge underwater. It rose high in the air, jackknifed for fifty feet, and came down in the water on the other side, never touching the bridge at all.

"I said to my boy, 'Son, that water's really moving. We better go back and see if anything's happened to our place.' I stopped off at the Roseland Rescue Squad, on Route 151, and one of the men there told me that during the night cars had, indeed, slid off Route 29, some of them into streams.

"Everything at home was all right, and I knew Mother, farther up the hill, was all right, too. I thought I'd drive back down to the rescue-squad station and we could start setting up road barriers. My younger boy asked to go along, too, and I said O.K. By that time, though, it wouldn't be possible to reach the highway-department man and the situation was so out of hand that barriers seemed irrelevant—nobody could move very far from where they were—so my sons and I made a tour of 151 as far as we could go in each direction, and then returned home. It was about four o'clock, and the rain had practically stopped.

"Son, that water's really moving."

"There were some curious things about this storm. One was that a couple of hours after the rain had stopped the creeks were down, and the rivers were down in a couple of days. Another was that the people who didn't suffer any damage didn't know there had been anything unusual. They might have lost lights and phones, but storms often do that here. They come out of their houses after breakfast to drive out of the county to their jobs or otherwise go about their business as usual. But there was no business as usual in Nelson County that morning."

The principal grim statistics for Nelson County were: 126 people dead or missing, 92 bridges out, 250 houses and 700 or more automobiles swept away, and hundreds more houses and cars damaged. Personal-property damage was estimated at several million dollars. The road system was a shambles. The state of Virginia has one of the best-marked and best-maintained systems of roads in the country. The morning after the storm, reconstruction of the part of it in Nelson County looked impossible.

What is known as the Massies Mill section, in the western part of the county, had, generally speaking, the most rain. However, in the southern part of the county, near the junction of the Piney and Tye Rivers, Sheriff Whitehead said, a man left three tall, empty, uncovered steel drums in the back of his pickup truck on the evening of the nineteenth, and the next morning found them almost full, containing thirty-one inches of water. A July, 1942, storm at Smethport, Pennsylvania, set a world's record for the time involved, with 30.8 inches of rain in four and a half hours, and a total of 34.5 inches in fifteen hours. The reported thirty-one inches in the south of Nelson County thus closely approaches the total for the Smethport storm. Completely reliable data on rare and unexpected meteorological events, particularly those happening in remote regions, are difficult and sometimes impossible to obtain. Sheriff Whitehead's recollection of the thirty-one-inch figure is backed up by the statement of a Geological Survey man who went to Nelson County from Norfolk directly after the storm to interview residents and who also reported the thirty-one-inch figure—which is the one that appears in the Senate committee report. Regrettably, the Geological Survey agent did not retain the name of his informant, and the Weather Bureau, on later searches, was unable to locate him. All it could unquestionably verify was a fall of twenty-seven inches in the Massies Mill area. However, in the words of one of the Weather Service men to whom I talked, "This doesn't mean that thirty-one inches didn't come down in Nelson County."

In the Massies Mill community, which was named for an eighteenth-century gristmill and where early in this century several score houses were built for lumber-company employees, eighteen buildings were lost and forty-eight severely damaged. I drove over there to talk with Ned Bowling, a seventy-eight-year-old widower whose house had been so badly battered that it had had to be replaced. Bowling and I sat for a spell talking on the little front porch of his new, one-story house. "Yes," he said, looking right and left from his rocker. "I can count where ten, eleven homes once in eyeshot here aren't here any longer." He told me that during the big rain he had got up at two o'clock in the morning, but that his house had seemed dry and he had gone back to sleep. "At three o'clock," he said, "the water came into bed with me, and I went upstairs." Later that morning, after the water had receded somewhat, rescuers took him off in a rowboat. Much of the first floor of his house had torn loose and floated away.

Though the greatest amount of rain was recorded in Massies Mill, the Davis Creek section suffered the greatest loss of life. Davis Creek, a tributary of the Rockfish River, flows north through hilly country. Four miles above Lovingston, it can be reached by a road off which run lesser roads that often become mere tracks as they rise into the hills or descend into the hollows. Along there, Sheriff Whitehead told me, I would see a lot of evidence of the storm's work. I could also call on Miss Dora Morris, a seventy-six-year-old survivor, whose house, at the head of the valley below Roberts Mountain, is perhaps the most elevated building in the region. I was advised not to take my car, so one of Whitehead's deputies, Jack Saunders, drove me in a police car that was specially equipped for travelling rough roads.

The Davis Creek area is too inconspicuous a part of the world to have had much recorded history. People began living in the humblest sort of dwellings back in the hollows there not long after the county's first settlers arrived. In recent years, some one-story brick houses, rather imposing for Nelson County, had been built in the lowlands. As we drove alongside Davis Creek, now an inconsequential trickle at the bottom of an eroded bed a hundred yards wide, Saunders showed me where three of the brick houses had stood.

"They were right here where we're passing," said Saunders, a slight, alert middle-aged man. "The water just took these brand-new houses—whoosh!—and washed them away. And, of course, along with them, the people asleep or awake inside them. All this immediate vicinity, including the road right here, is rebuilt land."

Miss Morris's house, which we reached at the end of a track high up a hill, had nothing in common with the unfortunate brick ones. Built of unpainted clapboard, it was obviously old, and was large for that section, being two and a half stories high. On the way up there, Saunders pointed out to me great bare faces of bedrock on the sides of mountains, some of them a quarter of a mile wide and several times that long, whose mantle of earth had turned to liquid under the deluge and plummeted down.

Miss Morris's house, which she later told me had been built by her father a hundred years ago, had in front of it a large white-mulberry tree, numerous high, dusty-smelling boxwood bushes, and an astonishing number of metal containers of various sizes and shapes planted with a wide assortment of flowers. Also visible were two healthy, happy-looking dogs of part-setter ancestry, along with a score of chickens. In back, a more or less level plot of ground, partly shaded by an enormous walnut tree, stretched to a wide gully in which a branch of Davis Creek flowed. Near the trunk of the walnut tree was an iron pipe emptying spring water into a wooden tub—Miss Morris's water supply. Not far off, near the back of the house, was her fuel supply—piles of two-foot log quarters. Saunders, who is known to just about everybody in the county, introduced me to Miss Morris, who lives alone. She is a brown-eyed, intelligent-looking woman with a strong square face and a strong, square body reminding me, for some reason, of an Anglo-Saxon Golda Meir. We exchanged a few words about the storm, but none of the rather modest ones she spoke that day were as indicative of her sturdy independence as the first ones she uttered the morning after the rain. A helicopter, one of several assigned to relief work in the area, had set down on the flat beside the walnut tree, causing an uproar among her chickens, which had weathered the deluge in their house and, until a few moments before, had been foraging contentedly in the rain-flattened grass. A couple of volunteer rescue workers from the area stepped out of the aircraft, whose rotors kept whirring. One of them said, "Miss Dora, we've come to take you off the mountain." The other, moved by the local spirit called "funning," said, "Why, Miss Dora, surprised to find you. Heard you went chuting-the-chute last night down the mountain on a log."

"If the good Lord had wanted me off the mountain, I'd have gone down last night, on a log or off it," she said. "I appreciate your concern, but I'm not leaving. Now you boys get that flying machine out of here. It's scaring my chickens."

That first morning, and for weeks thereafter, the cleanup proceeded, and, to a lesser degree, it was still proceeding at the time of my visit. At its height, a command post was set up at Lovingston under the direction of Cliff Wood, an auburn-haired farmer of forty-three, who was one of the county's four supervisors. The county's churches—Baptist, Christian, Episcopal, Methodist, and Presbyterian—had opened their doors to house and feed the homeless. Looting was insignificant. Outside aid was sent from other parts of the state, from the federal government, and even from abroad. Among those who arrived to help were a couple of hundred members of the Mennonite Disaster Service, some of them from as far away as Canada and many of them trained in carpentry and other skills, who swiftly put their church's concept of the brotherhood of man into action. "They were marvelously quiet, disciplined, efficient, and productive," said Wood, who, by all accounts, had been quiet, disciplined, efficient, and productive himself.

A couple of weeks after the storm, the Nelson County *Times*, a weekly paper, published a letter from a man in a nearby county who had delivered numerous loads of emergency supplies in Nelson County right after the flood and had talked with numerous survivors. It said, in part:

> What is a flood like? It is like misery and death which no one can describe or attempt to describe.
> It's like a banker trying to save his records and seeing a big wall of water break the glass in front and having to be taken out by boat. It's like hearing the big wall of water hit the back of your restaurant and reaching to pull all the switches, run and have a man drown in your place at twenty-five minutes to four the morning of August 20, 1969. It's like a woman telling you through sobs and tears that they had lost everything her family and family before them had worked for all their lives. It's like living on top of a hill and going out to check the stock at three in the morning and having to wade through water up to your knees. It's like living on the side of a mountain and seeing water, rock, trees and everything coming down at you with no place to go. It's like your house gone along with everything that you have except what you have on your back.

Nature's energy and man's had, nevertheless, done a great deal to rehabilitate Nelson County, Hughes Swain, the county agricultural agent, told me while I was there. The work of moving much of the runaway earth back to where it belonged went on through the winter after the storm and by 1971, I later learned, between 85 percent and 90 percent of the damaged agricultural land was back in production. The county game warden told me that there seemed to be as many wild things in the forests and meadows as there were before. The evidences of the storm most visible to motorists passing through the county when I was in it were weathered-gray accumulations of stumps and dead trees, some of them twenty feet high, piled by the watercourses. By now, even these probably have begun to blend with the landscape.

7

State Bird

Two decades ago, when Indian summer came to Central Park, so did the eastern bluebird (*Sialia sialis*). From time to time, with gentle, undulating flight, it could be seen migrating southward among the trees or pausing for a while to rest in their branches. Northward in the spring it was rarely visible there, journeying then to its nesting sites by a more westerly route. Now few, if any, bluebirds pass through the Park in autumn. The species seems to be in one of its cyclical periods of scarcity, perhaps the worst since records have been kept.

126

It is somewhat odd therefore, that, in the midst of this decline, Governor Rockefeller in Albany on May 18, 1970, should have signed a bill making the eastern bluebird the official bird of the State of New York. Actually, the signing constituted a minor historical event. For, at a stroke of the Governor's pen, the nation, for the first time since its founding, had an official avian symbol for every one of the component states. The bluebird joined a select group of twenty-nine species representing the other forty-nine states, some of which have birds in common. Seven eastern states share the cardinal, the bird most heavily favored; six western states have the meadowlark; and five in Dixie claim the mockingbird. New York shares the eastern bluebird with Missouri. A second bluebird, the mountain bluebird, is the choice of another pair of states, Idaho and Nevada. There is no confusing the two birds, however. The eastern bluebird is a low-land dweller with a reddish breast and a cheery warble, while the mountain bluebird's feathers lack any touch of red. Normally the mountain bluebird stays at altitudes above a mile high and is, except at dawn, a remarkably silent creature.

State birds are usually selected for their historical associations, economic value, or beauty of song. Alabama, for example, chose the flicker because its yellow, black, and red feathers were the colors worn into battle by various men of the state's contingents in the Civil War. Utah's California gull rendered crucial service to the earliest Mormon settlers during the first spring after their arrival; it devoured hordes of locusts that were eating the first crop of grain as it sprouted. And South Dakota's ring-necked pheasant—not a native, in fact, but a bird of Asiatic origin—annually draws to the state thousands of hunters who leave there large quantities of money.

Ordinarily, state birds are adopted by acts of legislatures or gubernatorial proclamation. A few, however, have become official by tradition or other means. The brown pelican, the largest state bird, whose wingspread is an awesome nine feet, is considered Louisiana's state bird because it adorns the state seal, approved in 1902. This is also the method by which the bald eagle has come to be the official bird of the United States. In 1782, Congress voted to put the eagle in the country's Great Seal.

Action on state birds has typically been initiated by a state's Federation of Women's Clubs, aided and abetted by conservation groups and public-school authorities. The decades of the 1920s and 1930s were an especially active time—thanks in large measure to the considerable energy of Mrs. Katherine B. Tippetts, of the General Federation of Women's Clubs, in Washington, D.C. At her suggestion, women's clubs in states lacking an official bird placed the names of favorite birds on informal ballots, which were distributed as widely as possible, particular attention being paid to the schools. "The state bird itself is really less important than the thoughts and discussion involved in its selection." Mrs. Tippetts has said. A number of states had already set aside a Bird Day for study and appreciation, and the state-bird vote was commonly announced on Bird Day.

New York's first Bird Day was on April 2, 1915, an occasion that in due course (as environmental study broadened) was incorporated into Arbor and Bird Day, Arbor and Wildlife Day, and in recent years has become simply Conservation Day. The bluebird won the informal referendum that was held on Bird Day, April

13, 1928, in a campaign under the direction of Mrs. Charles Cyrus Marshall, of the New York State Federation of Women's Clubs. Runner-up was the robin, honored today as the state bird of Connecticut, Michigan, and Wisconsin. Official action usually follows the popular vote within a year so, but the bluebird languished as New York's unofficial bird for forty-two years, the longest unofficial state-bird tenure on record. A decisive move to correct this situation was made the spring of 1969, when Mrs. Allen Christopher, of Marathon, in Cortland County—traditionally excellent bluebird terrain—telephoned the office in Albany of her assemblyman, Mr. George Michaels, of Auburn. She asked him to do something about getting legislation passed to make the bluebird's status official. Mrs. Christopher and her husband, who run a home-and-garden supply store, are active amateur ornithologists and had just finished attending a convention of the Federation of Bird Clubs of the State of New York, held in Marathon, where the longstanding neglect of the bluebird had been noted with more than a little asperity. Michaels explained that it was too late to introduce a bill in 1969, but promised to do so the following year.

True to his word, at the next session Michaels set the machinery in motion. In the Senate, he got Senator Tarky Lombardi, of Syracuse, to handle the bill, which became S.6245. It was passed on February 18th by a vote of forty-nine ayes and no nays, eight senators being absent or excused. Final legislative action took place on March 2 in the Assembly. Mr. and Mrs. Christopher had seats in the chamber when Michaels, wearing a bluebird pin on his lapel, rose to introduce the measure. At first he was unable to make himself heard over a barrage of cheeps and twitters from both sides of the aisle, but, having surmounted this difficulty, Michaels launched into his endorsement and, to applause from the chamber, introduced Mrs. Christopher, noting that three of her forebears had served in the Assembly. "Ladies and gentlemen," Michaels said, "in order to make Mrs. Christopher's happiness complete, I implore you to give this bill your unanimous support."

All did not go quite as smoothly as it had in the Senate, however, An opponent materialized. Seymour Posner, Democrat of the Bronx, arose and said, "Mr. Speaker, I have some misgivings about this particular bill." He pointed out that city dwellers, of which he was one, knew the sparrow and knew the pigeon. "But I think it is premature to talk about the bluebird," he said, "because, very frankly, the bluebird is not a bird that is well known. Who has seen a blue jay—bluebird, whatever they are—who has ever seen a bluebird except on greeting cards, and people who live in rural America? People who live on the lower East Side and West Side and North Side and South Side—how are we going to go along with a bird we never saw!" Despite Posner's antagonism, however, the bill passed—104 to 1—and in due course the Committee on General Laws sent it along to the Governor. Those present two months later at the signing report that he affixed his signature rapidly, with no outward show of emotion.

Assemblyman Posner had a point, however. It is, as a matter of fact, highly unlikely that most people who live in this city will ever see a bluebird, even should their numbers revive considerably—unless they journey to the American Museum of Natural History, where there is a mounted specimen of our state bird in a display titled "Birds of the New York Area." The reason a city dweller and a bluebird are unlikely to meet under ordinary circumstances is a matter of habitat.

New York State bird, male and female.

City residents tolerate crowding, noise, pollution, and the substitution of concrete for greenery. The bluebird, which is slightly larger than a sparrow and has a poor, round-shouldered posture when perching, prefers quiet and rural surroundings. It is, in effect a bird of another era. In the vanished Currier & Ives landscape of an America of long ago, when the ice was going from the lake and patches of snow still lay in the forest, the bluebird was the first to greet the plowmen venturing into their fields. A nineteenth-century poet described its coming as "a rumor in the air for two or three days before it takes visible shape." Its back the purest and most gorgeous blue, matching the cloudless sky, its red-brown breast the color of the awakening earth, the bluebird was the gentle symbol of spring for a gentler land. Three hundred and fifty years ago, it reminded the Pilgrims of the chunky robin redbreast they had left behind in England, and they called it the blue robin.

These days, alas, bluebirds cannot be called common anywhere, and they have been put on the Audubon's Society's "Blue List" of birds whose future seems endangered. Drastic scarcity was authoritatively noted in the winter of 1961-1962 by Dr. Douglas James, of the University of Arkansas, perhaps the country's foremost bluebird scholar. He wrote that the abundance then was less than 20 percent of normal, the lowest ever recorded in the annual nationwide Christmas bird census of the Audubon Society. (Most bluebirds fly south in winter, but quite a few have normally stayed on through the winter in all but the most northerly areas in this country and Canada.) The severity of several winters and cold, early-spring storms in the Northeast along the migration routes during this period had apparently wiped out the last bluebirds known to nest in New York City. Before that, several pair had regularly raised young each year in the woods of La Tourette Park, in the center of Staten Island, the adults cruising out over its golf course for insects, which they characteristically took either on the ground or on the wing. (Army worms, tent caterpillars, cutworms, and other pests are staples of their diet.) Bluebirds once nested in Central Park, but Richard Edes Harrison, the cartographer and conservationist, cannot recall any Manhattan nesters in the thirty years or more he has been birding here. Nor have any been spotted by members of the Linnaean Society in any of the other boroughs. John Bull, of the staff of the American Museum of Natural History, compiler of the authoritative *Birds Around New York*, agrees with this assessment.

If anybody could help me find a bluebird in the city of New York, I had been told, it would be Dr. Theodore Kazimiroff, a dentist who is the official historian of the Bronx, and an expert on the city's wild places. I called Dr. Kazimiroff one spring day, and he seemed optimistic. "There are even bluebirds on Hunters Island in the winter," he said. "I think they come down from Westchester to spend the cold months there. Usually they're to be found in a place called Sumac Grove. It has lots of berries and seeds they like to eat in the winter. Come up tomorrow, and we'll go over to Hunters Island and see if we can find any of the people who saw bluebirds last winter."

Hunters Island, which is not an island at all but a peninsula, is the most northeasterly section of Pelham Bay Park—itself the most northeasterly section of the city, and its second-largest park. I met Dr. Kazimiroff at his office and home, on East 201st Street, and we went to Hunters Island in his car. On the way over, he told me, "I used to see nesting bluebirds on the Huntington estate in the southern section of Pelham Bay Park every year a while back. The remains of an old orchard there gave them the nesting holes they love to live in. If only people buying places today with old orchards or shade trees wouldn't be so all-fired eager to fill the holes in them, then the bluebirds would have a better chance. Now they're gone from the Huntington estate. The Tallapoosa garbage dump stands there instead." Dr. Kazimiroff sighed.

In a moment or two, however, his good cheer returned. "The people we are going to see today are perhaps the truest nature lovers in all of New York City —the real, simon-pure enthusiasts," he said. "They come out to this remote park day after day the year round to little community camps they have built—a camp with people of predominantly German ancestry here, one of predominantly Greek ancestry there, and so on. They spend their time in the woods listening to the wind sough through the trees, or along the shore hearing the waves of Long Island Sound lap against the rocks. They are people of very modest means, but they love nature and they have hearts of gold."

We left his car at the Orchard Beach parking lot and started north along a deserted road to Hunters Island, whose trees were visible in the distance. After a while, we came to a one-story, red brick building, which, according to Dr. Kazimiroff, had replaced the Hunter mansion, a magnificent, colonnaded, regal manor house that had been built in 1840 and was sold to the Parks Department in 1877. "Presidents and royalty came to the mansion in its day," Dr. Kazimiroff said. "It had a fabulous art collection, including Titians and Rembrandts, that was eventually sold at auction." In front of the brick building at several wooden tables sat a number of plainly dressed men and women, eating from brown paper bags or playing card games. Dr. Kazimiroff recognized three or four and greeted them in German. Then he left the road and took a narrow path leading into the trees. Soon it brought us to a camp that was frequented, Dr. Kazimiroff told me, largely by persons of Russian background, and was near the Sumac Grove he had mentioned. The camp consisted of a crude wooden shelter or two, apparently for refuge from rain, some tables, old beach chairs, and an outdoor grate. Half a dozen men and a woman were present, all of them rather square in build with broad Slavic faces. Dr. Kazimiroff and the campers hailed each other vigorously in Russian, and then, speaking partly in English and partly in Russian, he inquired about the presence of bluebirds around the camp during the previous winter, making clear that he did not mean the large blue bird that is the blue jay but the smaller blue bird with the red breast that is the bluebird. The group's leader said firmly that the bluebird had been there all winter, but that none had been seen recently.

"What did I tell you?" Dr. Kazimiroff exclaimed. "Now they've gone back to Westchester."

Assuming Dr. Kazimiroff was right, I set about tracing the Hunters Island bluebirds (or at least some members of the tribe) to their nests. Parts of Westchester, I knew, are still certainly bluebird country. It retains sizable patches of open grassy space, hillside meadows, abandoned fields, and margins of thin woods —all of which bluebirds like. I lived in Chappaqua for a number of years, and used to see them there often, even in winter. So after my trip to Hunters Island, I asked the Sawmill River Audubon Society, whose membership is largely centered in Pleasantville and Chappaqua, to help me locate examples of our newly official state bird. A note in the Society's bulletin brought plentiful news of them. The closest to the city was in Silver Lake Park, adjoining White Plains, some twenty miles to the north, where a nest had been discovered. Other members told of regular sightings that, because of the season, presumed domesticity. Paul Frese, conservationist of the Westchester park system, reported a number of pairs in the Ward Pound Ridge Reservation, including some who had wintered over. And bluebird families occupied boxes elsewhere in the Pound Ridge section. Some had successfully raised two breeds of four fledglings each by early July. Boxes are important to the bluebird, because it is the only strictly hole-nesting bird that cannot make its own shelter.

Thus it depends on natural cavities or boxes with entries of less than an inch and a half in diameter to keep out large, unruly invaders like starlings. With the present vogue for filling tree cavities and eliminating old trees, bluebird lovers who wish to have the birds near them must largely depend on putting up boxes to attract them.

A great advocate of this practice, and perhaps the foremost bluebird lover in the entire state, is Mrs. Fujiko Matsumoto, who had lived in Chappaqua during some of the same years I did. The space in front and back of her house there, bristling not only with boxes but feeders as well, often seemed to be swarming with bluebirds. Her reputation was such that, in 1962, the magazine *Audubon* published an article on her and her year-round devotion to the birds. She took particular pains to see that their food did not freeze during the winter, and the cuisine was four-star—chopped beef heart, canned dog food, yellow corn meal, chopped cheese, suet, and meal worms that she raised for the purpose in her cellar. The diet may have been responsible for the fact that in 1954 one pair produced four broods in a single season. The feat, the magazine observed, had been pronounced "highly unusual" by a "stunned" ornithologist at the American Museum of Natural History. Mrs. Matsumoto's husband, Javius, an electrical engineer, had rigged up a way of keeping squirrels and other unwanted marauders out of the feeders by giving them a shock.

When the Matsumotos moved from Chappaqua in 1967, the rumor was that they left because the town was becoming too crowded for bluebirds. This was not quite the case, Mrs. Matsumoto told me in her present home, in Pawling, forty miles to the north, when I went to call on her there one day. "It's true that the town was becoming crowded. We had no bluebirds the last two years. But my husband was going to retire anyway, and we wanted more rural surroundings." Pawling provided them, and bluebirds, too. The Matsumotos were looking at some land there on a meadowed hill one autumn day in 1966 when a flock of migratory bluebirds settled into some trees on it. They bought the land immediately. "I knew we'd be happy there then, and we have been," she said.

I walked with Mrs. Matsumoto from her house to examine one of a number of bluebird houses on the open lawn. The small roof had been painted white by her husband to reflect sunlight and render those within more comfortable, but the nest was empty now. Mrs. Matsumoto told me that the second brood had flown a few days before. "They are back in the trees at present." she said. "Their parents may still be feeding them." The nest was a typical one, merely a mattress of dried grass stems piled into the box. The parents had started their second brood in it the first week in June and had departed in early July, the whole process having taken about a month. The eggs, light blue in color, of which there may be from three to six but are usually four, take twelve days for incubation. Seventeen to eighteen days later, the young exit from the hole in a flippety-floppety flight of from fifty to seventy-five feet. The fledglings have spotted breasts, like young robins. Both robins and bluebirds are thrushes, although the bluebird is not famous as a singer. The male's song is a mellow, gurgling *chewery, chewery,* repeated in what is one of the lowest-pitched voices of any North American songbird. Another deep voice is that of the Baltimore oriole (Maryland's state bird), but, of course, none of the songbirds can go as low as a real basso profundo like the great horned owl (nobody's state bird). Some female bluebirds also sing, but very softly. Mrs. Matsu-moto told me that each evening the male had been coming out of the trees and returning to the box to try to persuade the female to start a third brood.

On my way back to the city, late in the afternoon, I stopped at Chappaqua, where, at the top of Mountain View Road, according to report, there were bluebirds to be found. Sure enough, it was true. From among the tall trees that crown the site came a male's unmistakable sweet whistle. The more somber-colored female appeared first, alighting on an upper branch of an oak over the road where I stood beside my car. Then the male followed, still singing. He perched on a telephone wire high over the road, assuming his characteristic stoop-shouldered posture, and the evening sun caught his ruddy breast and made it ruddier still.

The sight gave me a moment of pleasure. I well remember, during my winters in Chappaqua, looking out on sunny days after heavy snows, when dripping icicles hung from gutters on my house, and seeing flocks of four or six bluebirds hover and daintly sip the water drops hanging at the ends of the crystal spears. The quick flutterings of bright blue and red against the piled white snow were a delight. May such gatherings of our state bird occur soon once again.

8

Bioluminescence

In the dusk of an early summer evening not long ago, my daughter and I walked beside the eastern wall of Central Park that runs along Fifth Avenue. In the dark spaces beyond the wall there came, now and then, small flickers of light—wee, pinpoint blasts that rent the soft shadow. Again and again they flashed sporadically —the pale, soft, disjointed artillery of summer's night.

"Oh, Daddy," said my daughter. "Fireflies! I didn't know there were fireflies in Central Park."

"Goodness, yes," I replied. "They live and breed there. They are probably the best-known example that we have of bioluminescence."

"What is bioluminescence?" she asked.

I tried to outline it for her very briefly. What follows is an explanation in greater detail.

Bioluminescence, the emission of light by living things, has puzzled and fascinated men throughout history. In the flickering of fireflies on summer nights, the glow of fox fire in the woods, and the dazzling displays by the tiny luminescent creatures of the ocean, ancient peoples saw something eerie, beautiful, and magical—a fire that burned but did not consume. Before it was understood, or even named, this cold light inspired poetry, engendered superstitions, and probably played a part in accounts of miracles, many of which refer to mysterious lights or strange effulgences. The first written reference to bioluminescence is found in one of the Thirteen Classics of China—the "Shih Ching," or "Book of Odes," which dates from sometime between 1500 and 1000 B.C. It contains the line "Glowing intermittenly are the fireflies." Perhaps a millennium later, Aristotle listed some examples of bioluminescence in the plant kingdom. In the first century A.D., Pliny the Elder noted that a Mediterranean jellyfish and edible mollusk (*Pholas dactylus*) shone "as if with fire in dark places, even in the mouths of persons eating them." Other early observations were made by such seventeenth-century scholars as Francis Bacon, René Descartes, Robert Hooke, and Marcello Malpighi, and, indeed, ever since their time bioluminescence has been not only a source of wonder but an object of scientific investigation. It is still not completely understood, but researchers now envision technological applications of it which range from detecting cancer to combating the smuggling of heroin.

Bioluminescence is distributed widely but very erratically through the ranks of life. Two large groups of plants—bacteria and fungi—possess it. As for the animal kingdom, bioluminescent organisms exist in almost half of its twenty-seven phyla, or major divisions. The organisms include such tiny creatures as flagellates, hydroids, and radiolarians, and such larger organisms as sponges, nemerteans (bright-colored marine worms), ctenophores (marine jellyfish-like animals), crustaceans, clams, snails, squids, centipedes, millipedes, insects, and fish—the only vertebrates among them. No amphibians, reptiles, birds, or mammals have the luster or scintillation of self-produced light. The highly unsystematic occurrence of bioluminescence among earth's flora and fauna has perplexed researchers for years. An organism that is bioluminescent may have close relatives that are not. The late E. Newton Harvey, who was Henry Fairfield Osborn Professor of Biology at Princeton from 1933 to 1959, described the anomaly in this fashion: "Imagine the names of all the forms of life written on a huge blackboard—the scores of phyla, classes, and orders descending from there to the hundreds of thousands of plant and animal species. Then imagine a man with a handful of wet sand standing off from the blackboard. He throws the sand at it. Where a grain sticks to a name, that species becomes bioluminescent—where not, no bioluminescence. The capacity really seems as disorganized and inexplicable as that."

All bioluminescence, whether its source is plant or animal, is an almost completely cold radiance. Less than 1 percent of the energy released in the chemical reaction producing it is in the form of heat—a level of efficiency that Westinghouse and General Electric would like very much to match, for even the most advanced fluorescent illuminating devices dispense their energy as 22 percent light and 78 percent heat, and incandescent light bulbs give off a range of 4 percent to

12 percent light and the rest heat. Blue is the dominant color of bioluminescence, but red, yellow, orange, green, and pearly tones also exist. The light stays within the visible range of the electromagnetic spectrum, having no infrared, ultraviolet, or penetrating radiation. Physically, except for the almost total absence of heat, it is no different from any other light. It can affect a photographic plate, can induce chemical reactions, and can be polarized—although its emission in polarized form by an organism has not been definitely established. Dr. Jean-Marie Bassot, a French scientist, believes, however that a small shrimp he has been studying—*Meganyctiphanes norvegica*, whose home is in the Scandinavian fjords and in the River Clyde, in Scotland —may emit light from several eyelike structures in its body in the form of a laser, which is a highly sophisticated form of polarization. A laser (the name is an acronym for "light amplification by stimulated emission of radiation") is a beam of light whose waves all travel in the same direction, as opposed to those of ordinary light, which vibrate in all directions. The first laser was produced in 1960, and up to now laser light has been thought of as a product of man's ingenuity, manufactured in a complicated optical device, not in a small shrimp's body.

By far the best-known example of bioluminescence, virtually all scientists seem to agree, is the firefly, a creature that inhabits every continent except Antarctica. There are more than 2,000 firefly species, of which 100 are known to inhabit the United States. The two that are most common in the New York area are *Photuris pennsylvanica,* which has a greenish light, and *Photinus pyralis,* which is somewhat smaller and whose light is yellow. Both, it is known, still breed in

Central Park, but their numbers have diminished, mainly because of the spraying of pesticides and the increase in human traffic through the Park. Human footsteps pack down the soil, thus reducing vegetation by denying air and water to the roots, and at the same time destroying many small tunnels and subsurface spaces. The vegetation is necessary to fireflies, because its roots provide for some of the tiny animals on which the firefly larvae feed, and the tunnels are the homes of these creatures and of the firefly larvae as well. One evening several autumns ago, when I was in the Park digging some dirt for my terrarium, I found a firefly larva near the Fifth Avenue wall, north of the Conservatory Pond. The larva was nearly an inch long, and as it lay in the dirt on my trowel, it reminded me of nothing so much as the fierce-looking dragon that used to emblazon the imperial banner of China. The creature had a dark, horny shell, rather weak multiple legs, small eyes, short antennae, strong, curved jaws, and two round lights glowing near the end of the tail. It had hatched some fifteen months before, four weeks after its mother, having mated, had laid perhaps a hundred eggs on or just under the surface of the soil. At its hatching, it was less than an eighth of an inch long. By day, it hid among the grass roots; by night, until the chilly weather came, it hunted. Largely by the sense of touch, using its legs and antennae, it located its food— mites, bristletails, and small snails and earthworms. With a poisonous bite, the larva paralyzed and partly liquefied its prey, and then it sucked in their substance like a nourishing soup. At the first frost, the larva hibernated under a stone, and during this period of reduced activity the lights in its tail were barely visible. Awakening in the spring, it more or less repeated the actions of its first summer. I took the larva out of the trowel and returned it to the damp soil. Its life cycle called for it to awaken again at the start of the next spring and to pupate in late May. If it did so, it used its legs to dig a shallow pit in the earth, which it roofed with strips of mud it had formed by chewing soil and extruding it as ribbons from its mouth. After ten days inside the chamber, metamorphosis was complete, and the newly formed firefly broke through the roof and started its search for a mate.

The most dramatic displays of fireflies to be found anywhere in the world occur along certain riverbanks in the Orient; several of the best-known sites are in Thailand. The scintillating shows have been objects of astonishment to Occidentals for nearly 300 years and of diligent study by some for several decades. In 1680, a Dutch physician travelling downriver from Bangkok wrote, "The glowworms . . . represent another shew, which settle on some Trees, like a fiery cloud, with this surprising circumstance, that a whole swarm of these insects, having taken possession of one Tree, and spread themselves over its branches, sometimes hide their Light all at once, and a moment after make it appear again with the utmost regularity and exactness." The description at once brings to mind a Christmas tree with flashing electric lights, and a more contemporary description does not alter this impression. An American scientist, Hugh M. Smith, making the same journey in 1935, wrote, "Imagine a tree thirty-five to forty feet high, thickly covered with small ovate leaves, apparently with a firefly on every leaf and all the fireflies flashing in perfect unison at the rate of about three times in two seconds, the tree being in complete darkness between the flashes. Imagine a tenth of a mile of river front with an unbroken line of *Sonneratia* trees with fireflies on every leaf flashing in unison, the insects on the trees at the ends of the line acting in perfect unison with those between. Then, if one's imagination is sufficiently vivid, he may form some conception of this amazing spectacle." Smith added that the rhythmic flashing is confined to male fireflies and "occurs hour after hour, night after night, for weeks or even months."

Such displays, scientists believe, represent communal, rather than individual, efforts to attract mates; the females are present, in and around the trees, but their lights, which are dimmer and are not synchronized, are lost in the concerted male blazes. These surprising performances, scientists have decided, make complete ecological sense. The country inland from the trees where they take place tends to be dense swamp, in which the individual flash communications that gild the summer nights in American fields would be largely obscured. A tree beside a river, on the other hand, is an assembly point that can be seen for hundreds of yards as it flashes like a huge torch under the nocturnal sky. Firefly breeding in the tropics, unlike that in our Temperate Zone, is more or less continuous. The mated insects withdraw to breed and die within a few days, but the supply of fireflies in and around the trees is steadily renewed. Recently, a scientist in Malaysia who was studying these glowing trees with the aid of a light-recorder attached to an oscilloscope discovered that the flashes of the species under study occurred once every second, lasted for only a fraction of that time, and were actually not single flashes but double bursts of light, spaced a thirtieth of a second apart, which were seen as one by the human eye. The fireflies' flashing in unison is one of very few instances of synchronism in nature, and its mechanism has lately received the attention of several investigators. At present, the investigators incline to the theory that, through the eye, the individual firefly's central nervous system judges the timing of the discharges by the majority of the fireflies in the tree, regulates its own flashing to that pace, and so locks into the cycle. The process is more or less like the sudden handclapping that occasionally erupts at sporting affairs, the controlling agent there, of course, being a sense of rhythm established (somehow) through the ear.

"Biotope" is a word that the general public is hearing more and more often in this ecology-minded era. Webster's Dictionary defines it as "a region uniform in environmental conditions and in its population of animals for which it is the habitat." By far the world's largest biotope is the deeps of the sea—below the level of a thousand feet. Its uniform environmental conditions are dimness shading into utter darkness, food scarcity, great pressure, great stillness, and great cold. Light vanishes just below its upper limit. Food, mostly in the form of dead organic matter from the sunlit upper realm, rains slowly down. The crushing pressure is hundreds of times that of sea level. A great calm prevails; the biotope is untroubled by the fiercest storms, whose effects extend downward no more than a couple of hundred feet. Many fish in these regions, in the absence of the stresses that occur in the upper sectors, have developed almost decalcified, paperlike bones. Only vast, slow-creeping currents, resulting from differences in temperature in the ocean as a whole, impart any movement at all to the water in the abyss. The chief instrument of motion is cold water, which, being heavier than warm water, sinks in the vicinity of the poles and flows away softly along the bottom to all latitudes, carrying with it the dissolved oxygen that is necessary to life. Temperatures through most of the biotope hover around the freezing point. A thousand feet beneath the top of the biotope, the human eye can see no light. From that level on, eternal darkness stretches through all the oceans of all the world. No day, only perpetual night. No summer, only everlasting chill. No dawn, no dusk, no spring, no fall, no seasonal change—only an infinite sameness. In this immense and forbidding habitat, most of the planet's bioluminescence is found. For centuries, scientists assumed the ocean depths to be no biotope at all. They were viewed as a desert, utterly devoid of life. In the 1880s, however, the net hauls of deep-sea-research vessels began to discredit this theory, and then it was discovered that the vast subsurface gloom was atwinkle and ashine with the cold fire of living things.

The investigation that firmly established the existence of large-scale bioluminescence in the depths was made off Bermuda between 1929 and 1937 by Dr. William Beebe, of the New York Zoological Society. As part of this effort, he descended repeatedly into the ocean deeps in a steel globe called a bathysphere, which was outfitted with fused-quartz portholes and a searchlight. On three occasions, he reached a depth of 3,000 feet. The bathysphere, suspended by a cable from a mother ship at the surface, was lowered and raised by machinery, and over telephone wires to the mother ship Beebe described his voyages into a realm never previously seen by man. First, he said, the red, orange, and yellow colors of the spectrum faded; at 200 feet they were swallowed up by green. Four hundred feet farther down, green was replaced by a deep, rich blue— a light that, Beebe found, was impossible to read or write by. This color, very familiar to divers, prevails at this depth because sunlight's blue wave lengths are the most penetrative in water. For reasons that still aren't known, most marine bioluminescence is blue. At 2,000 feet, Beebe reported, the water became jet black, and he turned on his searchlight. On a typical plunge, Dive No. 30, a few of the sights he saw, according to a stenographic record made at the surface, were sparks in all directions that faded, then burst anew; lovely, bright pale-blue lights close to the porthole; a big glow, six to eight inches across, rising in the distance; at the edge of the searchlight beam, ten or fifteen lights steadily coming and going; a three-inch-long fish lighted all over with a silvery luminescence; a flash of pale rose-red. The show never stopped.

Beebe's research is still the greatest effort ever made to sample deep-sea fauna in a restricted region. His descents were supplemental to a long period of netting, in which he made 1,500 hauls with a one-meter-wide net in an eight-mile circle south of Bermuda, to depths of 7,200 feet. He collected 115,747 individual fish, of 220 species. In 1966, when R. J. Lavenberg, curator of ichthyology at the Natural History Museum of Los Angeles County, was collecting between New Zealand and Chile, he brought to the surface 20,479 individual fish, of 154 species. Ninety-six percent of Beebe's individuals were luminescent, as were 98 percent of Lavenberg's, and two-thirds of the species obtained by each of the men were luminescent. The fantastic appearance of many of these fish, as their collectors and other scientists have described them, is such as to suggest demons painted by Hieronymus Bosch. Some of the fish have great heads, composed almost entirely of mouths filled with huge teeth, attached to relatively insignificant bodies. One, brought from a depth of 12,000 feet in the Pacific Ocean, has a sizable luminous organ, like a pod, dangling from the

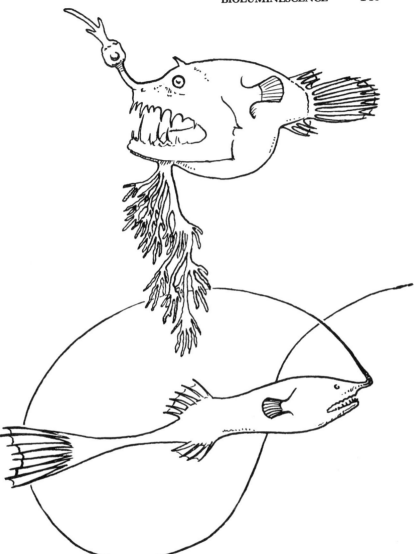

Strange bioluminescent creatures of the ocean deep. Above, the deep-sea devilfish, *Linophryne arborifer;* below, the deep-sea angler, *Gigantactis macronema.*

roof of its mouth. The angler fish has a light organ projecting from its forehead on a tentacle. The light organs of other species are on stalks, streamers, or pendants, or are embedded in the flesh in varied designs. Often these organs have as appurtenances a lens, reflectors, and pigment screens, making them into small lanterns. Another instance of a complicated luminous system is that of the hatchet fish, a disc-shaped creature about the size of a twenty-five-cent piece that lives in the upper range of the biotope. A row of bluish stomach lights running from its mouth to its tail are connected with ingenious light-reflecting tubes arranged so that the brightest light is directed downward and the softer tones shine up the fish's sides; the result is that the fish blends in with the surrounding water almost to the point of invisibility. Besides fish, Beebe identified in the searchlight beam and in the nets he brought to the surface numerous species of luminescent shrimp, squids, and jellyfish, among other shimmery creatures. Some years earlier, a squid raised from a depth of 10,000 feet in the Indian Ocean was found to possess bioluminescence in many colors besides blue. It had five light organs on each eyeball, eight on the underside of the body, and four on a pair of arms. The collector described it thus: "One would think that the body was adorned with a diadem of brilliant gems. The middle organs of the eyes shone with ultramarine blue, the lateral ones with a pearly sheen. Those toward the front of the lower surface of the body gave out a ruby-red light, while those behind were snow-white or pearly, except the median one which was sky-blue. It was indeed a glorious spectacle."

Deep-sea research has advanced considerably since Beebe's time. In studying underwater luminescence today, scientists use a light detector called a photomulti-

plier tube, which is so sensitive that when it is lowered
into the depths it can pick up light intensities as low as
a trillionth part of full sunlight. The detector, on steel-
armored conducting cables, has descended more than
12,000 feet. In every area tested and at almost every
level, bioluminescent flashings have been noted—some
of them mass-produced, lasting for several seconds, and
approaching the radiance of moonlight. The detector
has also shown that the eyes of depth animals respond
to fainter lights in their environment than the eyes of
human beings do. This fact was demonstrated by monitoring the movements of the sonic-scattering layer,
which is the name that oceanographers have given
huge aggregations of minute animals, mostly crustaceans and mostly light-producing, that form broad
thick sheets in the ocean. (The appellation arose from
the fact that these sheets of living creatures were im-
penetrable to the sonar waves used during the Second
World War by Navy patrol ships to locate submarines.
Once a submersible was under the layer, it was safe
from detection. Owing to the improvement of sonar,
this circumstance no longer obtains.) Sonar devices
and light detectors have shown that the sonic-scattering
layer rises and falls hundreds of feet during a twenty-
four-hour cycle. It is deepest—perhaps as deep as half
a mile—at noon on clear, sunny days, and it rises to its
highest point, within a hundred feet of the surface, on
nights when clouds obscure all moonlight and starlight.
Let a break in the clouds occur and only a little radiance
from the stars trickle through, and the sonic-scattering
layer reacts, sinking a bit. Under similar submerged
conditions, the human eye, of course, would not react.
The greater sensitivity of the eyes of abyssal fish and
other depth creatures has also been demonstrated in
anatomical studies, which show them to possess a not-

ably larger amount of photosensitive pigment than
man's eyes do. The sonic-scattering layer's vertical migrations are thought to be a survival mechanism by
which its members can avoid predators and yet spend
a portion of each day in the food-rich upper layers of
the ocean, where photosynthesis takes place.

There are bioluminescent displays, often stunning
in their splendor, at the surface, too. The bow waves of
ships passing through the Red Sea at night have been
known to trigger acres of blue-green flame that circle
the vessels over and over. Such displays are caused by
the excitation of hordes of dinoflagellates—tiny, one-
celled creatures that can kindle upon the surface of the
sea streaks of oozy lightning or sheets of chilly fire.
It was from these creatures, which are red by day, that
the Red Sea got its name. (The poisonous red tides that
have occurred in Florida, killing many fish, are produced by an unrelated, non-bioluminescent organism.)
Bioluminescence is sporadic in the Red Sea, but it can
always be found in four bays in the West Indies—three
of them in Puerto Rico and one in Jamaica. There a
boat crossing at night provokes the resident dinoflagellates to glitter with such power that a person sitting at
the stern will have no trouble reading a newspaper by
their light. Unhappily, much of this luster is now
threatened by pollution. Off the Bahama Islands, surface displays of bioluminescence are provided by the
mating ritual of the marine fireworm, an inhabitant of
the area. A few days after the full moon, during much
of the year, the female of the species rises from her
burrow on the bottom about an hour past sunset, blaz-
ing brightly. Her presence attracts males, and a furious
circling ensues, during which both eggs and sperm are
emitted in a strongly luminous cloud.

Many other things glimmer and glow just under the

surface. Sea pens are polyps living in colonies, the individuals of which have featherlike heads atop stalks that fasten them to the bottom. When they are stimulated at night by waves or passing fish, light suddenly undulates over the colony, passing from one to another. Louis Agassiz, the great nineteenth-century naturalist, wrote that they shine at night with a "golden green light of a most wonderful softness." In the Banda Sea, at the remote eastern end of the Indonesian Archipelago, live two extraordinary species of fish—*Photoblepharon* ("light eyelid") and *Anomalops* ("strange eye"). Both species have under their eyes large, constantly bright light organs that, by different methods of screening, seem to turn on and off rhythmically. Professor Harvey, of Princeton, who studied the fish in their habitat almost half a century ago, found that the light of both is created by colonies of luminous bacteria that live in the light organs and receive a rich supply of blood and oxygen from the host. Whether the bacteria are present in the egg or enter the light organs at a later stage is a mystery that scientists have yet to solve.

Although the ocean is rich in bioluminescence, fresh water decidedly is not; in fact, no large body of fresh water contains any bioluminescence. Close relatives of bioluminescent marine forms remain dark in fresh water. To date, the only known bioluminescent fresh-water organisms are a New Zealand limpet, about the size of a kernel of corn, that eats algae and clings to rocks, usually in swift-moving streams, and the larva of a firefly which lives in tropical pools and breathes by tracheal gills.

Bioluminescent organisms that have their homes on land include springtails, centipedes, millipedes, beetles, and those members of the plant kingdom which gleam with self-manufactured light—certain fungi and bacteria. The most striking individual among the animals is the *ferrocarril*, or railroad worm, of Central and South America. The adult female and the larvae of both sexes have eleven pairs of greenish-yellow lights along the sides and a red light at the head. At night, the moving worms resemble tiny railroad trains. Another brightly lighted bug—a West Indian click beetle sometimes called the *cucujo*—changed the course of history in a minor way. In 1634, a British fleet intended a night landing on Cuba. The cautious officers in charge of the enterprise withdrew, however, when they saw countless bright lights moving about on the shore, in the belief that these were torches carried by regiments of Spanish soldiers; actually, they were *cucujos*. A sight that rivals the firefly trees of Asia is furnished by New Zealand glowworms—small larvae of a species of fly, masses of which live in caves, where they glimmer blue-white overhead. The glowworm attaches itself to the ceiling of a cave in a transparent tube, from which it drops lines bearing tiny beads of adhesive; these trap insects, which it then hauls up to the tube and devours. The beauty of the assembled worms is such that on North Island, near Waitomo, the site of the largest glowworm caves, a tourist industry has arisen, complete with a hotel and guides. The guides lead the tourists through the dim grottoes, warning them against all talk, for noise causes the larvae to dim or extinguish their lights. In full glory, the largest cave presents a sky never seen above the earth—a sky packed almost solid with galaxy after galaxy of blue-white stars.

The bioluminescence of plants differs greatly from that of animals. Instead of being sporadic or rhythmic, it is a continuous, steady glow. In fungi, either the mass of fine fungal threads or the fruiting body, or both, may glow. Dead wood of any kind—tree stumps, fallen logs, moldering leaves—may display this fungal light, popularly known as fox fire. Occasionally, fox fire has been associated with the supernatural. American Indian legends of ghost bears returned from the spirit world were inspired not by apparitions but by flesh-and-blood bruins that had enjoyed a daytime nap in a rotting hollow log and then, with strands of fox fire clinging to their fur, had gone for a nighttime amble through the woods. The smallest lamps known are found among bacteria, the other group of plants containing bioluminescent species. Only one twenty-five-thousandth of an inch across in some cases, the bacteria are so tiny that the light of an individual cannot be seen with the naked eye. That of colonies, however, is readily visible. Light-producing bacteria live in the air all around us and in salt water. Dead fish or squid stranded in a tidal pool overnight usually glisten with them. In fact, before the days of antiseptic surgery luminous bacteria frequently sprouted on mending wounds, and Civil War doctors visiting the hospital wards at night noted that these wounds seemed to heal more quickly than others, the bacteria evidently consuming waste tissue. The glow of bacteria is soft and spectral. An early investigator of bioluminescence computed that if the dome of Saint Peter's in Rome were lined with a single layer of luminous bacteria they would emit a light so diffuse that it would be equivalent to that given off by a single tallow candle. When such bacteria are packed solidly together, however, they are capable of much more impressive displays. Another early investigator filled a number of twenty-five-liter glass flasks with a salt-water variety and put them on display at the International Exposition in Paris in 1900. They gave off a blue-green light so strong that visitors could easily read by it and could recognize acquaintances twenty or twenty-five feet away.

The first concrete advance toward an understanding of the workings of bioluminescence came in 1667, when the English scientist Robert Boyle discovered that air was necessary to make the light—that the glow of fungi and bacteria faded and disappeared in a vacuum. Some sixty years later, the Frenchman René de Réaumur demonstrated that dried or powdered luminous organisms would glow with the mere addition of water, and thus that the light-producing matter was inherent in their substance. But the greatest early step was made by another Frenchman, Raphael Dubois, in 1887. By experimenting intensively with hot- and cold-water extracts of Pliny's clam, *Pholas*, he showed that its light came from two materials, both of which he named after Lucifer, the light-bearer. One, which could not be damaged by heat, he called luciferin; the other, which was destroyed by heat, and which he judged, correctly, to be an enzyme, a class of compounds that generally react in this fashion, he called luciferase. Both were needed for the production of the clam's light.

Early in the twentieth century, Professor Harvey arrived on the scene, dedicated to collecting and classifying all bioluminescent creatures and to mastering their anatomy and chemistry. For nearly fifty years, he was the world's leading authority on bioluminescence. Shortly before he died, in 1959, at the age of seventy-one, he observed with pride: "Today my students have had their students; and these students have had theirs. I call these my first-, second-, third-, and fourth-generation bioluminescent descendants." Over the decades, he showed that luciferin and luciferase were the main light agents in many bioluminescent animals besides *Pholas* but that these substances were usually specific for each animal; they were interchangeable only occasionally, among close relatives. When Beebe was making his Bermuda studies, Harvey, a friend of his, joined him for several weeks in 1930 and, while he was there, proved the existence of luciferin and luciferase in deep-sea animals. Much of Harvey's work was done with *Cypridina*, a small marine crustacean living off the coast of Japan. When *Cypridina* is disturbed, it discharges through several glands two secretions whose luciferin and luciferase, upon mingling with the water, give off a soft bluish light. In the Second World War, when Japanese troops were too close to the enemy at night to use a flashlight for map reading, they produced a substitute light by pouring water over a palmful of dried *Cypridina*. Harvey spent years trying to fathom the precise chemical nature of *Cypridina's* light agents, but he was not completely successful.

Dr. William D. McElroy, one of the most famous of Harvey's pupils, was the first to discover the exact chemical formula of a luciferin—that of a firefly. The formula turned out to be $C_{11}H_8N_2S_2O_3$. He and his team of researchers also studied the firefly's luciferase, which proved to be a euglobulin, or protein that is insoluble in water, and to be so complex that it had a molecular weight of 100,000. They could not synthesize it, as they had the luciferin, but they isolated and crystallized it, and were thus able to use the natural substance in experiments. The work represented years of dedicated effort at Johns Hopkins University, where McElroy was a professor of biology. He says that what actually occurs in the nerve-controlled flash of the firefly is part of the ordinary process of anabolism and catabolism, jointly called metabolism. To understand this process properly, one must realize that the energy by which all life, in any form, is carried on depends upon an organism's taking into itself nutritive material, rearranging parts of the material for its own use, and discarding other parts. The most elementary nutritive materials are the inorganic matter and the solar radiation taken in by plants. What the plants make out of them constitutes, directly or indirectly, the nutritive materials on which the almost countless forms of animal life depend. The nutritive materials are handled in a highly complex fashion, whether in a self-sufficient unicellular organism or in a multicellular one in which many types of specialized cells make a contribution to the functioning of the organism as a whole. The incredibly diverse cell components that process the nutrient materials have not yet even been counted, and the full range of their activities is far from being known. They normally act in a matter of milliseconds, producing within the cell a continuous cycle of chemical buildup, breakdown, buildup, breakdown of nutritive materials. This biochemical fluctuation fuels life. It continues in the organism without interruption, millions of times an hour, until the moment of death.

To man, of course, the firefly's flash is the most noticeable part of that insect's life process, and it neatly exemplifies the rhythm of chemical buildup and breakdown—of anabolism and catabolism—within the insect's light-making cells. According to McElroy, the substances involved in the buildup phase are adenosine triphosphate, or ATP, the molecule that in all organisms is the storehouse of energy for vital operations; luciferin; the enzyme luciferase; magnesium, which chemically binds the ATP to the enzyme; and oxygen, which enters the cells through a network of tracheal tubes. In the breakdown phase, they are adenosine monophosphate; oxidized luciferin; the enzyme luciferase, which remains unchanged; the magnesium, which also remains unchanged; inorganic pyrophosphate; carbon dioxide; water; and the flash of light. McElroy inclines to the belief that the nerve in this nerve-controlled process does not actually turn the light on with periodic nervous impulses. Rather, he thinks, during the nocturnal periods of flashing the nerve maintains what could be called an open circuit to the cells, and the light is turned off by an inhibitory product of the breakdown phase and then, when it disappears, during the buildup phase, is turned on again by the open nerve circuit.

Plant luminescence, of course, is not controlled by nerves, and McElroy thinks that the steady glow of bacterial light is a side product of the organism's metabolism. He believes that the chemistry of this light, which has been fairly well studied over the years, is very much like that of the firefly's luminescence. The luminescence of fungi has not been investigated sufficiently to enable anyone to hazard an opinion on the chemistry involved. A few organisms have been found whose bioluminescent systems do not appear to be based on luciferin and luciferase. One is the Pacific jellyfish *Aequorea*, a creature whose umbrella, measuring from three to six inches across, is rimmed with light organs that give off a bluish-green luminescence in response to mechanical or chemical stimulation. In this system, a single protein component emits light in the presence of calcium, according to Dr. Frank H. Johnson—another famous pupil of Harvey's, now a biology professor at Princeton—who has been studying the jellyfish for more than a decade with a colleague, Dr. Osamu Shimomura.

The uses of bioluminescence to an organism are

not always clear. In some cases, of course, the function is obvious. In the firefly and the marine fireworm, it serves to bring the sexes together. Those deep-sea squids and shrimp that eject a luminous cloud into the water apparently use it to help them escape from their enemies. But in the matter of function there is a large gray area and a large black one. In the first, some of the things that scientists assume—so far, without proof —are that the light organs dangling in or near the huge mouths of abyssal fish serve to attract prey; that the often intricate patterns of luminescent structures on fish and other creatures furnish recognition signals, keeping similar individuals together and thus helping to preserve the species; that deep-sea fish may use luminescence to see by or to delineate territory with; and that the hatchet fish's strange illumination system is for camouflage. In the black area, even Harvey could not explain the value of light to a fungus or to unicellular organisms that float on the surface of the sea, blown hither and yon by winds. Some scientists doubt whether there is any. Johnson has written, "Luminescence is certainly of questionable value to the jellyfish *Aequorea.* Apparently, it lacks organs of photoreception, and therefore cannot detect visible light from other individuals of its own species or from any other source. The same seems to hold true for the fungi, the bacteria, and many protozoa."

If McElroy's theories are accepted, however, much of the mystery surrounding the uses of bioluminescence and its erratic appearance in life's plan is cleared up. Late in 1971, I had a talk with him in Washington, D.C., where, following his years of bioluminescence research at Johns Hopkins, he was ending a three-year term as director of the National Science Foundation prior to assuming his present post of chancellor of the

University of California at San Diego. "Scientists believe that life made its appearance rather early in the 4.5-billion-year history of the earth—probably 3 billion or 4 billion years ago—and most likely in the form of single-celled, ocean-dwelling creatures," he told me. "The atmosphere then had virtually none of the free oxygen it has today. Instead, it's thought, the atmosphere was reducing; that is, it was one in which hydrogen, by far the most prevalent substance in the universe, was the main element in chemical compounds. The first organisms, therefore, were anaerobes, whose metabolic activity is carried out through fermentation in the absence of oxygen, their nourishment coming directly from the basic chemical elements or from simple organic molecules, such as rudimentary sugar compounds. Gradually, over geologic time, the amount of free oxygen in the atmosphere increased, and penetrated into the ocean. This occurred by several routes, including volcanism and lightning discharge, but mainly through photolysis, the breakdown of water molecules into their constituent hydrogen and oxygen, after which the hydrogen, being lighter, tended to escape from earth, and the oxygen accumulated slowly in the atmosphere. This oxygen would have been downright poisonous, to anaerobic organisms that could not get rid of it quickly, and the easiest way to do so would have been to convert the oxygen into water by combining it with hydrogen, which could have been obtained by breaking up a hydrogen compound. Enough energy would thereby have been liberated in single packets, or quanta, to excite organic molecules to emit light. Support for this notion comes from the fact that virtually all luminous reactions can detect and use oxygen at extremely low concentrations. For example, bacteria, a type of primitive life that may very well have occurred in the primeval seas, can easily produce measurable light even when the oxygen concentration is as low as one part in a hundred million. During subsequent evolution, life forms evolved that could use oxygen directly in their metabolic machinery. But those organisms that already had bioluminescence did not lose it easily, because it was part of their primitive heritage. Thus, in their case, bioluminescence represents a vestigial system in organic evolution. I should say that in the more advanced organisms bioluminescence came at a much later evolutionary stage, in a wide variety of often unrelated species. Among many of these, light emission has been adapted to fulfill definite functions. The firefly is an example. So is the deep-sea squid. Where it was beneficial, it has been preserved; where it was non-injurious, it has been tolerated." McElroy's theories, which he worked out in conjunction with a Johns Hopkins colleague, Dr. Howard H. Seliger, have manifest advantages. Not only do they explain the apparently useless emission of light by forms far down the evolutionary ladder—including lowly creatures that dwell inconspicuously in the sea, such as the sea pens and hydroids—but they also account for the random occurrence of bioluminescence in the higher forms.

Technology these days is expanding into more and more areas, and one of them is bioluminescence. Researchers are attracted by the purity and sensitivity of the bioluminescent reaction. "Bioluminescent materials are very specific and reliable," McElroy has said. "Once you have isolated them from any organism, a steady light results when you mix them together with the appropriate chemicals, such as ATP and magnesium." This is true, furthermore, even when they are present in almost infinitesimal amounts. Harvey discovered that *Cypridina*, his crustacean, has luminescent material so reactive that one part of it to 40 billion parts of water produces a flash discernible to the dark-adapted eye. By contrast, the most dilute solution in which any dye is visible is one part to ten million.

One basis for the use of bioluminescent materials in technology is the fact that luciferin and luciferase react to ATP, the substance common to all life. When luciferin and luciferase are placed in measured amounts in a solution or compound to be tested, the resultant light or lack of it proves the presence or absence of living matter. Moreover, the quantity and brilliance of the light obtained indicate the relative amount of living matter present and its state of health; sickly cells are not as reactive as healthy ones. This new field of research has been aided greatly by the recent development of highly sensitive rapid recording devices for the measurement of light. In theory, scores of applications of this bioluminescent reaction are possible, and some have already proved workable. For example, two Maryland chemists received a patent early in 1971 for the employment of firefly extract to determine the presence of cancer; in cancerous cells the light from the extract dims. A test for urinary infections that is hundreds of times as fast as any previous tests (which all required from twenty-four to forty-eight hours) has also been found: firefly extract from which the ATP has been removed reacts with the ATP of the infecting bacteria, producing light. The National Aeronautics and Space Administration at one time considered the use of firefly extract to find out whether there is life on Mars. The assumption behind the proposed experiment—Project Diogenes—was that ATP is common to all solar-system life. A probe would have picked up Martian soil and mixed it with firefly extract that lacked ATP, and any light produced would have been registered on a tiny photomultiplier tube and flashed to earth by telemeter.

Researchers have found that mutant strains of bioluminescent bacteria can be bred to be sensitive to many substances. In 1970, New York City received a federal grant of almost $100,000 for the development, in collaboration with a West Coast company, of mutant strains of salt-water bacteria that would be sensitive to heroin, which, like every other substance, gives off effluents into the atmosphere. One purpose of the project is to create a strain of bacteria that could be used to monitor ports and airports through which heroin is brought into the city. The project is currently proceeding, under the direction of the Mayor's Criminal Justice Coordinating Council and the Police Department. Evaluation of the method was still going forward under the direction of the West Coast company and the Police Department at press time.

Valuable uses are foreseen for aequorin, the protein from the jellyfish *Aequorea*, because it produces light when it is combined with tiny amounts of calcium. "The discovery of this property opened the way to a new method for the microdetermination of calcium in biological systems with the advantages of sensitivity, specificity, and speed," Johnson has said. "The sensitivity extends in principle to better than one-billionth of a molar of calcium in a small volume. Its specificity is solid. Its reaction speed requires at most a few milliseconds." In eleven years' work with ten tons of jellyfish, Johnson and Shimomura have isolated only a small part of an ounce of aequorin, but they hope that they will eventually be able to produce an artificial equivalent of it. This artificial product could then be used by hospitals to make quick measurements of calcium levels in the blood and by public-service laboratories to determine the calcium content of milk and other fluids. Moreover, aequorin is almost as sensitive to strontium as it is to calcium, so it could also be used to detect and measure radioactive strontium in fallout. "Bioluminescence," McElroy told me, "has recently become an astonishingly valuable quantitative tool for biochemical and biophysical investigations."

During most of the time that life has existed on earth, bioluminescence has twinkled and gleamed, mating the fireflies, lighting the oceanic abyss, forming phosphorescent waves as a soft ornament to tropic nights. Now such phenomena have fallen under the scrutiny of technology. With this development, who can predict the future of that twinkle, that gleam?

9

Newly Discovered
Animal Species

On the western side of Central Park, covering an area of
several square blocks, stands the American Museum of
Natural History, within whose walls work scores of
scientists eminently knowledgeable on the subject of
life forms, both dead and alive. Conservationists and
other nature lovers, I know, have understandably
been concerned about the number of animal species
that have become extinct since man's record-keeping
began—as well as those that in the very near future
threaten to follow in their footsteps. Such publications

as the federal Fish and Wildlife Service's *Rare and Endangered Fish and Wildlife*, dealing with mammals, birds, amphibians, reptiles, and fishes of this country that are now considered in jeopardy, and the International Council of Bird Preservation's *Red Data Book*, whose several thousand entries in three categories ominously notes the global avian species that are extinct, endangered, and rare are merely two instances of this solicitude, which seems to be growing each year.

Lately, however, while pondering this circumstance, I got to wondering about input at the other end of the spectrum: whether, in other words, man was also adding to the list of animals already known by the discovery of new ones. The work of finding, classifying, and naming new species is largely carried out by museums of natural history whose staff members mount expeditions to far-off places, where they collect and bring back for study biota they regard as new or interesting. Since the American Museum of Natural History is one of the largest and most active anywhere, I decided to take my question there for an answer. The Museum's public-affairs office made, in advance, the necessary arrangements with those who could help me, the curators of most of the animal sections, and some months ago I spent several days at the Museum talking with these people. I had barely begun before it became clear that new animal species are coming into man's knowledge every year at a rapid rate. In point of fact, new arrivals may range from a few annually into the low thousands, depending on the grouping being considered. And progress would be even faster, I was told, were sufficient manpower available to dig into the backlog of suspected new species, specimens of which lie awaiting examination in the Museum's drawers, cabinets and files.

If one accepts the count, published a few years ago, by Ernst Mayr, director of Harvard's Museum of Comparative Zoology, in his book *Principles of Systematic Zoology*, there was a shade more than 1 million known animal species existing at that time. They included, of course, all things considered animal, from the protozoa, which are one-celled, sometimes microscopic forms (some 28,000 species) to the largest and heaviest of our planet's critters, the whales and the elephants. These behemoths are numbered among the mammals, whose species totaled 3,700. For my purpose, I disregarded the protozoa and the very smallest invertebrates, the mesozoa, and concentrated on those manifestations generally considered by the average person to be recognizable animals—the larger of the invertebrates and the vertebrates, the general designations that make up the animal kingdom in toto. Invertebrates constitute 94 percent of today's known animal species, with the overwhelming majority being composed of insects. The ascertained number of these in Dr. Mayr's list comprise three-quarters of a million. Among other invertebrates with sizable totals were the gastropods, most of which are shell-bearing mollusks (80,000 species); the bivalves which, besides the oysters and clams, include many other things (20,000 species); and the arachnids, the majority of which are spiders (57,000 species). The 41,700 species of vertebrates, the backboned animals, higher on life's ladder than the backboneless ones, have the fishes as the most numerous members (20,000 species). Birds are second on the Mayr list with 8,800 species and reptiles follow with 6,300 species.

Jerome G. Rozen, Jr., bearing the title of Ph.D., as did all my informants, was the first person I talked to. Rozen is curator of one of the insect divisions, as well as the Museum's recently appointed deputy director for research. Since I wished to start in the most populous animal area, that of the insects, Rozen was a logical choice. Being curator of Hymenoptera, an extensive insect order that includes the bees and wasps, he was at home, of course, in entomology and, as an administrative official, he had, into the bargain, an overview of the Museum's resources.

"Our various insect collections contain 14.5 million specimens," Rozen told me, "and among them are some leaders in the field. There is the Emerson termite collection, the world's largest, containing 94.7 percent of the named species, and the Kinsey gall wasp collection, which is almost equally complete. Kinsey, the investigator of sexual behavior, you know, was an eminent entomologist before his interest shifted (or narrowed). Then, stepping outside of insects, there is our spider collection with more than a million specimens, another world leader. And, of course, I could mention numerous others in the Department of Entomology and, indeed, in most of our departments dealing with various aspects of zoology. Parts of them are constantly being sent out for study to museums, the strongholds of taxonomy, which is the science of species identification and classification, and to universities as well, which devote some time to this. And, of course, the collections are used, too, by our own scientists. The work, though slow-moving, is important because until we can name an animal and place it in relationship to others we do not know its part in the scheme of things. We all know that life forms are intimately interconnected. But we can't, for example, truly judge the effects of insecticides on the environment until we know just as truly the role of its inhabitants. But, oh, what gaps we face! I could show you two-thirds of the insects in the forest on top of the Palisades just across the Hudson River whose habits and life cycles—and therefore their benefit or harmfulness to man—are unknown. Yet progress here goes slowly because qualified specialists are relatively few, while accumulations to be examined are large. I would say, for instance, that in our own insect material of 14.5 million specimens somewhere between one-third and one-half are unidentified and unnamed. The specialists aren't born yet who are going to clean up this accumulation. However, in the whole insect field the number of discoveries annually runs into the hundreds or into the thousands. The year 1952, I happen to remember, produced almost 7,000 new discoveries. When these eventually cease, some zoologists speculate that the most numerous animals will have been found to be nematodes."

Next I talked with Charles A. L. Cooke, at the time of my visit the arachnid curator, who informed me that between 1940 and 1966 something more than 1,300 new spider species had been discovered and named in North America alone, a figure that works out to an average of a bit more than fifty a year. Moreover, hundreds of new species are waiting to be described. Again, the bottleneck is a lack of qualified specialists, a situation even more acute with arachnids than with insects, Cooke said. At present, 40,000 spider species have names but because of a grievous overlap through the years Cooke suspected that they represented only half that many species. "Nevertheless, I surmise the world fauna is many, many times that," he told me. "When I collected in central Africa some years back, every specimen of the hundreds I brought in was something new. As for the rest of the arachnids, those that are named run into the tens of thousands; those that exist are probably mind-boggling."

One of the more interesting spiders found in this country recently was the brown recluse, named in 1940. Not until 1957 was the spider, originally confined to our south central states, recognized as dangerous to man. Since then it has spread northward to a larger area, principally through man's agency, mostly by way of motor vehicles. "If it gets into a heated building in the north, it is likely to survive," said Cooke. "Some have been found in New York City. Their bite is not lethal to man, as that of the black widow spider occasionally is. But it is a nasty one, causing what doctors describe as necrotic arachnoidism. This is a gangrenous lesion, in the case of the recluse usually a sore two inches across and very hard to heal." One victim not long ago, the actress Anna Kashfi, who is the former wife of Marlon Brando, was nipped on a yacht off the California coast and underwent skin grafts to replace tissue disintegrated by the venom.

William K. Emerson, the chairman and curator of the Department of Living Invertebrates, saw me next concerning mollusks, whose 50,000 species constitute his speciality. Mollusks are the things that, with the exception of crustaceans, are popularly called shellfish and include, among other things, clams, limpets, oysters, snails, mussels, and whelks. Each year a couple of thousand mollusks, aquatic and terrestrial, are discovered and named, Emerson told me. "Just visit an area that scientifically is poorly known, such as Somali, or the coast of China, if we ever get the permission to explore there, and you'll find new mollusks," he went on, "just as we surely would on the continental slopes offshore and in the deep ocean bottoms, whose fauna, too, are poorly known."

A dearth of qualified specialists also plagues Emerson's field, he told me, and it has created at least one

mildly humorous situation. "Scientists entering bio-
chemistry or molecular biology in such numbers these
days in preference to systematic biology have unquestioned opportunities to do important work and to add
greatly to the sum of man's knowledge. But their lack
of information of the whole animal can be embarrass-
ing. One biochemist who had ground up a number of
sea anemones found one possessing a potentially important antibiotic substance. But he didn't know the
creature's name. He had to go to some trouble to track
down a systematist to find it out."

Besides existing animals, natural-history museums by definition of function collect and study, as far as
possible, all forms of life that have ever occurred, a vast
assemblage, produced over the earth's eons of time,
which may, some scientists think, outnumber present
forms by an order of many million. One such example
of these was a genus of living cap-shaped mollusks
named *Neoplina*, belonging to a group thought to have
died out in middle Paleozoic time some 370 million
years ago until, as was reported in the public prints a
while back, a specimen was dredged up in deep water
off the western coast of Costa Rica. With the discovery,
one more animal thought to be extinct entered living
fauna. I asked Emerson to tell me something about this
retrieval from the past. "I could tell you a bit, but why
don't you see my colleague, Roger Batten, curator of
the Department of Invertebrate Paleontology, who
knows a lot more? Let's see if he's in," said Emerson,
reaching for the phone. Batten was, and I went to his
office.

"The mollusk," he informed me, "was named *Neoplina galathae* after the Danish oceanographic ship
Galathae that brought it to the surface in 1953 from
sandy gravel 5,000 meters down in the Pacific Trench

off the western coast of Costa Rica. It was described in *Nature* magazine in 1957. Fossils of its family were described in 1884. We think the mollusk may have changed its way of life during its recent history. All signs in the Paleozoic point to its acting like a limpet, that is, using its single, cap-shaped shell to cover its foot, which adhered to a rock in the shallow, warm water of its ancient habitat. Those were the days of epicontinental seas, shallow oceans overlaying continents with bodies of warm water, creating a climate in and out of the water that worldwide was very similar. Today we have the largest amount of emergent land that has ever been known, the work of continent-shaping separation through the slow shifting of gigantic plates on and just under earth's surface, creating new oceanic deeps. The deeps, among other things, cause warm and cold oceanic currents, resulting in a variety of climates, quite different from the climate of the shallow, epicontinental seas. In the climate of its deep habitat today, which is relatively free of predators, the mollusk seems to live with its shell on the bottom and its foot pointed upward to catch the rain of food falling down from the sunlit zone above, a complete reversal, in other words, of its former mode."

I left the realm of the invertebrates after this talk and entered that of the vertebrates, a region where man stands at the top of the heap, above thousands of his near and distant relatives, all of which jauntily sport a backbone. My first interview here was with Richard G. Zweifel, the chairman and curator of the Department of Herpetology, the heading under which the museum groups the amphibians and reptiles. Their worldwide fauna has 2,400 known species of amphibians and 6,000 known species of reptiles, Zweifel told me. "Scores of new species of both are being found each year," he said, "being about equally divided between the two classes. The tropical rain forests across the earth, in such places as South America and New Guinea, are probably the main repository of most of the land species remaining unknown. Zoologists tend to wince when they learn of a new road being started in these areas. For soon follows primitive man, who tills the soil by slash and burn, a technique that completely wipes out the old environment, taking with it perhaps thousands of as yet unknown insect species as well as higher forms of life. This is one reason why collectors garner more than they can describe right away, and why undescribed specimens pile up in the drawers and jars of the museum."

In addition to zealous collecting, an increase in sophisticated scientific equipment has enabled biologists to make discoveries of new species. "For example," said Zweifel, "another herpetologist, James Menzies, and I traveling independently in New Guinea in 1968 and 1969 studied a number of two-inch-long tree frogs of extremely variable coloration, their skins variously combining shades of green, brown, and gray. Previously, these were all thought to be of the same species. However, we caught their voices in the forests on portable tape recorders. Taking the tapes to our laboratories we subjected them to the scrutiny of a sound spectrograph, a machine that can draw pictures of the sounds that were on the tape. The machine showed that the calls of the three were decidedly different despite the fact that to the human eye the frog's morphology was identical. Thus our advanced sound techniques showed the three frogs, formerly masquerading under one name, clearly to consist of three species, none of which would interbreed with another."

Fishes are backboned animals that spend their lives

in water and from it breathe air by means of gills, Donn E. Rosen, chairman and curator of the Ichthyology Department told me. "Their worldwide fauna now numbers 20,000 species," he went on, "with a hundred new species a year being uncovered. Most of these just now come from the deep sea or the Amazon basin. Recently the latter has been contributing more. However, there are frequently even some new ones from the United States. Surprising, yes. But this is the case. From an area that one would expect by now to be totally known, of course. My guess is that ultimately there will be 30,000 species of fishes described. This is based on the fact that the hundred new discoveries a year doesn't taper off but remains steady, and we assume a large undiscovered reserve in the deep sea. But the fine-tooth-combing, even in supposedly known areas when using new techniques, can be profitable. Since 1963 I have been working the freshwaters of Guatemala, regions generally thought to have been pretty well covered. I go in and out of the bush by helicopter, a trip that takes less than two hours compared with the two weeks that it formerly took by mule train. Some of the most interesting places are isolated river valleys. It is the saving in time by aerial transportation, allowing more fieldwork, that produces improved results. Of sixteen valleys that I intend eventually to explore, I have done eleven so far. The five trips have produced twenty-two new species, which are related to the guppy and the pirana, among others, and vary from eight inches long to less than an inch when adult. This is comparable to the average length of all the fishes in the world, which amounts to six inches."

Cartilaginous fishes (sharks and rays) are the primitive ones in the fish category. They are so primitive, in fact, Rosen told me, that a spiny fish like the well-known striper is more closely related to man than to the sharks, a statement that may well surprise some members of *Homo sapiens.*

A specimen of another fish, the coelacanth, belonging to a group thought to have become extinct in late Mesozoic time 70 million years ago, emerged a little over a decade back, to enormous journalistic fanfare. It came from the deeps of the Indian Ocean off the Comoro Islands, where native fishermen knew the species. Its scientific recognition, like that of the mollusk *Neoplina*, increases the recorded living fauna by the number of one. This coelacanth now is included in the fish collection at the Natural History Museum. Since the first capture, three or four dozen more have been caught in and out of the Indian Ocean.

Birds are, as a class, more widely and faithfully observed by the nonscientist than any other animals. Hundreds of thousands of avian watchers bloom around the world, and their activity becomes ever more dedicated. Devoted surveillance by amateurs has turned up a few new species, though most watchers live in an area where the birds are well known. Although museum people thought for a while the supply of new birds species might completely dry up, this has not been the case thanks to the jungle recesses of Amazonia and the isles of the South Pacific. Professional ornithologists usually manage these days to add two or three new representatives a year to the roughly 8,800 known species of birds, Dean Amadon, the chairman of the Ornithology Department and its Lamont curator of birds, told me. In the decade, 1956-1965, for example, thirty-five new species were described, Amadon said, of which one was an Indian Ocean petrel and another a fourth species of Australian crow. Some of these will undoubtedly prove to be only "sports," or races of other species.

Amadon himself contributed two of the new finds, both from the Philippine Islands, one, a rail, a short-tailed, dun-colored, chickenlike bird about eight inches long, described with Kenneth C. Parkes, and the other a new genus, as well as a new species, of babbler, a bob-tailed, olive-green and yellow songster about the size of a wren.

Mammal species, whose ornaments include man, number at present approximately 4,000, said Richard G. Van Gelder, chairman and curator of the Mammalogy Department, when I dropped by his office. "However," he told me, "in contrast to most of the other animal divisions, this figure is decreasing through proper description. The reason is that in the great heyday of mammal discovery, from 1870 through 1920, expedition after expedition, some financed by wealthy hunting enthusiasts, roamed in game country, especially over Africa. The sportsmen shot or collected by trapping and brought back scores of creatures, which were described and named, some improperly or incompletely. For example, we now find that some of the supposedly different species from the east and west coasts of Africa actually belong to the same species."

While on balance there is a diminution of mammal species at the moment, some offset occurs through the discovery of new ones. In the case of existing mammals, this usually amounts to three or four a year. "We are finding these days many new ground-dwelling fossil species in the Caribbean region, whose lives apparently ended not long after Columbus arrived," Van Gelder said. "We blame the rat. Islands just now seem to be the best source for new mammal species, whose representatives for obvious reasons tend to be small. Among the several described last year was a red-backed mouse, with tail about four and a half inches long. This was found on an island of Japan, and, in addition, there was a brown, insect-eating bat two and a half to three inches long from Martinique."

One of the last large mammal species discovered, and a big one, was the kouprey, or forest ox, found in the jungles of Cambodia in 1934. The first specimen, a young animal, was brought to the Paris zoo. A mature bull stands six feet at the shoulder, is black with white stockings, and has formidable-looking, cylindrically shaped horns. In 1940 a study estimated the number of kouprey in its limited sylvan range in southeast Asia at 1,000. In light of what has been going on over there recently, the population, if there still is one, is probably substantially reduced.

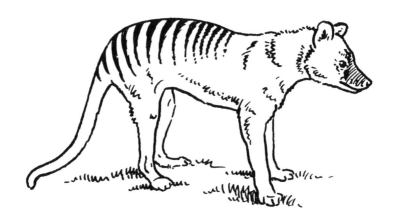

The thylacine.

Another large mammal, about whose existence there had been a question for the past forty years, may yet be found, after all, to have survived, Van Gelder told me. This is the thylacine, or Tasmanian wolf, the largest living carnivorous marsupial, a primitive form of mammal that carries its young in a pouch. The thylacine resembles a dog and is restricted to Tasmania. Its buff coat is marked with sixteen to eighteen dark chocolate stripes across the lower back, from which comes the alternate name, Tasmanian tiger, by which the thylacine is sometimes called. An adult measures six feet long from nose to tail tip. The last one officially shot was in 1930; the last zoo specimen died four years later. However, an intensive search for the thylacine is taking place in Tasmania's wild northeast and northwest sections, where scientifically corroborated tracks and scientifically uncorroborated sightings have been reported over the last twenty years.

With the end of my talks at the Museum, the question that had taken me there was quite clearly answered. New animal species from all the worldwide macroscopic fauna were entering man's records at an average rate that closely approximates 10,000 a year. Nor does there seem to be any reason to believe that this figure will lessen substantially any time soon. In fact, when the full count is in sometime in the indefinite future, several scientists at the Museum hazarded a guess that the total may well be three times the present sum of roughly 1 million species.

10

Beaver Defender

The Central Park Zoo, the delight of children and (sometimes) of their parents, boasts an exhibit of beavers (*Castor canadensis*). Last fall, after watching for minutes with absorption the antics of these furry animals in their pool, I returned to my office some blocks to the south. There on my desk, routed by an editor

180

conscious of my attention to nature, was an eight-page pamphlet printed on green, recycled paper titled *The Beaver Defenders*. Upon inspection, the periodical turned out to be an undiluted plea for appreciation and protection of *Castor canadensis* which, from the information set down in the paper by the editor, Mrs. Hope Sawyer Buyukmihci, is one of the most interesting and valuable but currently oppressed members dwelling within the world of North American living things.

My interest piqued by Mrs. Buyukmihci's prose, I determined to try and learn more about this obviously dedicated lady and the animal for which she had mounted her singular crusade. After a matter of weeks, this came about.

Mrs. Buyukmihci (whose name is pronounced Bew-yuk-muk-chuh in the unaccented Turkish fashion) is the wife of a Turkish-born metallurgist, who is now an American citizen. After our meeting, I can truthfully say that she is one of the beaver's most devoted champions in this country or, for that matter, anywhere else in that creature's extensive range north and south on our continent.

Mrs. Buyukmihci lives inside Unexpected Wildlife Refuge off Unexpected Road near the town of Buena in the flat, sandy, scrubbily forested part of southern New Jersey. A sweet-faced, kindly lady in her early sixties, she stands five feet three inches tall and, at the time, weighed 110 resolute pounds. In 1970 she founded The Beaver Defenders, an organization that now has more than 500 members in this country and Canada, who each month in return for a $3 annual subscription fee, receive a copy of *The Beaver Defenders*. At least one of its margins invariably bears the legend, "They Shall Never Be Trapped Anymore," since a prime objective of Mrs. Buyukmihci's work is to stop the trapping of beavers. The newsletters also contain ecological information, and stories and poems about beavers, such as the following from a New Jersey grade-school teacher titled "Trappers Beware":

> We're setting a trap for humans.
> We hope they take the bait.
> We want to captivate their hearts
> Before it is too late.

The newsletter's press run is always increased by several hundred over the number of subscribers in order to mail free and unsolicited copies to individual lawmakers across the country, including the entire legislative body of the State of New Jersey, in an attempt to get their cooperation in halting the trapping of beavers instantly, an effort that so far, alas, has met with little success. This fact, however, doesn't daunt Mrs. Buyukmihci in the slightest. Prior to 1970 and the formation of The Beaver Defenders, there was an eight-year period in which Mrs. Buyukmihci devoted herself to fashioning a warmer and warmer acquaintanceship with beavers. It was months, though, before she actually saw any of the creatures engaged in their activities in the woods and waters of the refuge, for beavers are extremely shy after years of ruthless trapping and hunting by man. Characteristically, however, Mrs. Buyukmihci persisted, often spending nights, many of them frosty, in pursuit of this aim, which eventually resulted in her overwhelmingly winning beaver trust. In the process she found that eventually she was able to feed and pet beavers, and to be privy to certain (as she describes them) enchanting beaver family sounds—the mother's warning hiss to the kits, the latter's kittenlike mews, the mother's childbirth cries through the walls of the lodge and her gentle murmurs after the kits are born. One midnight, when the thermometer was below zero, Mrs. Buyuk-mihci heard a wild, beautiful chorus of song coming from within a lodge. "It was a sheer paean of joy," Mrs. Buyukmihci said. On another occasion, wearing a swimsuit, she entered a beaver pond in search of additional beaver rapprochement. She may be the only person recorded in history thus far to have carried the quest for beaver friendship to such lengths.

The beaver, for its part, is the northern hemisphere's largest rodent, and the only mammal anywhere to have a flattened, scaly tail. It uses this, which is a foot long and six inches wide, as a rudder when it swims at speeds of up to four miles an hour, as a scull when swimming more leisurely, as a sit-down prop on land when gnawing trees, and, lastly, to create a community warning signal, striking the water with it to produce a sharp crack that causes every beaver in earshot to dive. Beaver hearing is remarkably acute, far better than man's, a fact which, coupled with a sense of smell as keen as that of any dog, considerably delayed Mrs. Buyukmihci's coming to friendly grips with them. To illustrate the sharpness of these senses, several decades ago a Rocky Mountain camper who had a pet baby beaver, heard, as he was preparing supper, its wail, like that of a frightened child, just before it plunged into a stream fifty feet off, barely ahead of the snapping rush of a coyote. The nearest beaver pond was a quarter of a mile upstream; yet in less than five minutes two beavers appeared from that direction swimming low and cautiously in the water and sniffing the air, to be joined almost immediately by another from downstream. All emerged from the water and smelled the bank where the coyote had been. It was well the predator had departed. Beavers are effective and, if possible, communal fighters in defense of young, as the well-bitten and often drowned carcasses of lynx, bobcats, and wolves have testified. Normally, though, beavers flee trouble. They mate for life, which is usually fifteen to thirty years, and, when full grown and sitting up, reach to about half of Mrs. Buyukmihci's sixty-three inches. Old fat ones that actually equal her weight of 110 pounds have been caught, but characteristically an adult scales just over forty.

Females bear two to seven kits, usually four, which arrive ordinarily in the spring following a four-month gestation period. The infants come into the world fully furred, active and open-eyed, weighing under a pound, and measuring some fifteen inches in length, of which three and a half inches is tail. A beaver family consists of the parents, the kits, and the young of the previous year known as yearlings. The latter depart in their third spring to take up life on their own. The family home is a roughly conical lodge, built of sticks, mud, and rocks, ten feet or more in diameter, which rises some four feet above the level of the beaver-made pond. Underwater entrances lead to its scrupulously clean interior with sleeping and plunge platforms above an indoor pool into which even new kits excrete, the waste resembling pressed sawdust. John Colter, the discoverer of the Yellowstone area in Wyoming, escaped hostile Indians almost 200 years ago by hiding inside a lodge. Beavers construct a lodge after damming a stream until a year-round pond at least two or three feet deep is formed, a level that protects them from virtually all predators except man. They tow cut logs and branches two to six feet in length to the lodge for use as building material, swimming with tail and powerful webbed hind feet and using the smaller dexterous front paws to hold the logs or to carry rocks and mud to fill in the chinks between them. This is the same type of construction they use for building dams. When not carrying objects, the front paws are held tight against the chest while swimming. The lodge is thinner at top for ventilation but strong enough there to resist even the pawings of bear. Inside, the beaver family feels safe, subsisting during the winter on a submerged raft of logs cut earlier and embedded in the mud nearby. Their four long, orange-colored incisors, their principal tool and weapon, can take down a willow tree five inches thick in three minutes. Back of the incisors a membrane closes in front of the throat, allowing the beaver to cut underwater. Molars for chewing bark and wood, its tougher food, are back of the membrane. When stripping bark from a two-foot branch, a beaver turns it round and round with the front paws like a man nibbling corn on the cob. Beavers also eat water lilies, fungi, aquatic plants, and algae.

Valves in a beaver's nose and ears close automatically underwater. Its eyes are better in that element than in air, having built-in goggles formed by thin membranes drawn over the eyeballs. An extra large liver that filters out impurities in the blood, a high metabolic tolerance to carbon dioxide, and an oversized lung capacity enable the beaver to remain submerged for more than a quarter of an hour and then to surface, if it wishes, half a mile from the spot of its dive. To accomplish this a beaver's internal functions slow down perceptibly underwater to reduce the drain on the heart and oxygen supply.

When the white man came to North America, the supply of beavers seemed inexhaustible, their numbers for the continent having been estimated at more than 400 million. Then they were diurnal and spent considerable time sunning themselves atop their lodges, combing their rough outer coats with the hind feet, each of which has a split claw ideal for this purpose and waterproofing the long hairs with applications of castor, an oil from a gland near the groin of both sexes. This situation, idyllic from the beaver point of view, did not last long. "A pogrom began," said Mrs. Buyukmihci. "Beavers became nocturnal, living like refugees in their own country." The reason was trapping, which was intensified when Beau Brummell in England started a vogue for beaver hats, a fad that spread to this country, as well. Hairs of the soft inner coat of the beaver are barbed and make a highly workable and resistant felt. Beaver hats wore almost forever and thus made sartorial sense. Early last century, however, the winds of fashion changed. Silk then became the desirable material for men's headgear, and the beaver boom was finished. But, by then, the beaver was, too, almost. Its low point was struck around the year 1900. Beaver were then practically extinct in this country east of the Mississippi River; only a relatively few scattered pockets of population remained elsewhere in the United States.

Now the beaver is on its way back. Restrictive legislation and the transference of live animals from places where they have survived to former haunts have seen a remarkable increase in beavers in the last few decades over much of the country. At present in the Northeast, every state in New England, with the exception of Rhode Island, has colonies. New York is well supplied and so is Pennsylvania, not to mention New Jersey. And the trend over much of the rest of the country is also to a distinct proliferation of beavers. If Mrs. Buyukmihci has her way, the trend will continue.

Her attachment to beavers began in 1962, the year after a return from her final stay in Turkey. She, her husband Cavit, a medium-sized, slender, handsome Moslem, and their children, a son and two daughters ranging then in age from fifteen to ten years old, moved from a small farmhouse in New Jersey to eighty-five acres of woods and streams, the nucleus of the present 260-acre refuge. The tract was bought because both husband and wife were nature lovers, a direction in which they hoped to lead the children, and also because Cavit had found a job forty miles to the north, an easy automobile commute. A three-room cabin, which the family has improved and expanded, stood on the land facing an old beaver pond with a vacant, disintegrating lodge. The sight of the lodge and a growing interest in the species sparked by Mrs. Buyukmihci's introduction to the colorful beaver writings of Grey Owl, the Canadian naturalist of forty years ago, made her start a determined search for beavers on the property. Its intensity mystified her family. The children at first were unsympathetic, to say the least, their frequent remark being "Beavers, beavers, that's all you talk about." Her husband, on the other hand, if puzzled, was more relaxed, accepting her quest as the will of Allah.

For days during the first summer Mrs. Buyukmihci strode determinedly among the refuge's maple, gum, sassafras, and oak trees and beside bodies of water looking for beavers or their signs. Then, in the early autumn, she came across a beaver dam, blockading a stream. But was it, like the lodge, old? Checking regularly, she one day found fresh mud in chinks between the sticks. Elated, she stepped on the dam—jumped up and down. It was solid. Rushing home, she passed the glad bulletin to her family. "They're here!" she announced. The family took the news calmly.

Thereafter, Mrs. Buyukmihci saw beaver footprints in mud, came upon the spearlike butts of gnawed saplings and trees that are signs of beaver handiwork, and heard from time to time sharp slaps of tails on water. But not for many months did she see a beaver. In an attempt to overcome their wariness, she took her husband's suggestion and fed them, carrying bundles of cut poplars, a beaver staple, to the scene of their activities and staying not far from them all night long, wrapped in blankets. In the morning the poplars were gone, but she had seen no beavers. Many vain evenings were spent thus. She stopped her vigils only when ice had locked in the stream.

The next spring when the ice had melted she renewed the feedings. The beavers continued receptive but remained invisible. Despite Mrs. Buyukmihci's best efforts, spring passed and summer arrived without sight of her quarry. However, late one July twilight, when she was seated near the beaver dam, she saw an unmistakable beaver swimming cautiously toward her, so low along the stream's surface that only the top of the nose, eyes, and small ears protruded. Taking advantage of a log on the other side of the waterway, it unobtrusively crossed the dam and headed downstream, a row of silver bubbles marking its underwater path. Mrs. Buyukmihci was overjoyed. She had seen her first beaver.

July became August and, although Mrs. Buyukmihci religiously continued her daily watch, the days passed beaverless. Late that month, though, the situation changed. Again, as the evening light was waning, she seated herself not far from the dam after depositing her load of poplars near it. As the dusk closed in, she tried to read some of Thoreau's writings. While doing this, she heard a small gurgle. Looking up, she saw that a broad, black nose had emerged from the water nearby. It belonged to an adult beaver and was coated with the algae scum which forms on the surface of backed-up waters at that time of year. The beaver only a few feet off climbed from the water, chose a stick of poplar from the pile near the dam, and ate the bark by nibbling it off corncob fashion. Then it took a second stick, and swam away with it. "With this trusting perform-ance," said Mrs. Buyukmihci jubilantly, "I knew that the beaver had seen me many times before, and had come to accept me."

Mrs. Buyukmihci has not the least trouble differen-tiating beavers. This one, which she later learned was a female, she named Whiskers. Beavers are difficult to sex, but Whiskers' enlarged breasts for nursing each spring proclaimed her femininity. Her mate, which also appeared before too long, Mrs. Buyukmihci named Greenbriar. Hoping to allay their fear and accustom them to her voice, Mrs. Buyukmihci started talking to them. One evening, to her great satisfaction, Whiskers replied. After Mrs. Buyukmihci had made some opening remarks to Whiskers, who was back of a clump of sweet-pepper bush munching on shrubbery, the beaver responded with a plaintive, questioning murmur. "She was asking," said Mrs. Buyukmihci, "is it safe to come near you? You won't hurt me, will you?" In return, Mrs. Buyukmihci answered reassuringly. Whiskers thereupon moved closer and continued eating. As Mrs. Buyukmihci returned up the trail toward her house, she could hear the contented snip-snip of Whiskers' jaws. Mrs. Buyukmihci said she has seldom felt happier.

Thereafter, her beaver-watching intensified. With the beavers having come to accept her, if not as an ac-tual beaver then as a heaven-sent food provider, Mrs. Buyukmihci was able to glimpse bits of beaver life that captivated her. She found that beavers bit snarls out of their fur like cats, and that young beaver kits find diving hard. Their fine, fluffy fur tends to hold them up like a kapok life preserver. The first brood of Whiskers with which she became acquainted she named Goldie, Brownie, Nippy, and Fluffy. She heard them mew when hungry like kittens, yet the sound had an unmistakable beaver quality.

A highlight of her beaver-watching occurred one December night just before all moving water fell entirely to the grip of ice. The temperature was eight degrees above zero and falling. "I could hear the groan of the ice near the shore contracting as the mercury plunged—violent, ripping noises like canvas being torn by a gigantic hand," she said. As the moon rose, she sat huddled near the lodge. Water still flowed over the dam, but the channel was growing narrower by the minute. "Around the submerged food raft, the moon showed me white bubbles clinging to the ice's underside, where beavers had gradually released their breath while gnawing underwater. I crouched on the bank, rigid as a stone. Around me the tortured ice continued to snap and growl. Then all at once I heard something completely unexpected in such bleak surroundings: the joyous voices of young beavers, snug in their winter lodge. Muted by the thick walls, first one melodious tone, then another, reached me. To this duet was added a third voice, then a fourth—vocal music at its best, a quartet humming in exquisite harmony. For a few moments, I forgot the stark scene before me—the desolate swamp and the frozen lodge. Fancy carried me to a springtime orchard where bees hummed and a warm sun shone. Suddenly, in the midst of this music, turbulence erupted below the dam, and I was startled to see Greenbriar pushing through the water. With a rattle of broken ice he hauled himself onto the dam. In the dim moonlight he looked as big as a bear. Lowering his head, he began to gnaw. By the guttural sound of his teeth, I realized he was grinding ice away to keep a channel open while water swirled black and swift around him, almost washing him off his feet. It was a moment of vivid contrast—the squat, powerful male figure intent on protecting his lodge where, in warmth and comfort, his children sang at their play."

Another indubitable highlight was when Mrs. Buyukmihci took to the water with beavers. Her companions were four kits, with whom she had made friends, youngsters who were just about weaned and swimming without parental supervision. The event occurred on a cold, drizzly July evening. Mrs. Buyukmihci, after reaching the pond near their lodge, called the kits. One appeared, his head lying watchful on the water, which is the animals' habit when they first surface in the presence of a friendly human being. Therefore, Mrs. Buyukmihci laid her clothes on the bank and stepped into the water, wearing a two-piece bathing suit. The adolescent floated some distance off appearing, naturally enough, quite puzzled by what was going on. Mrs. Buyukmihci moved to the deep part of the pond. The water there stood above her waist. "The little beaver eyed my progress doubtfully, I must admit," Mrs. Buyukmihci said. "As I crouched shivering in the cold stream he moved forward slowly, disappeared, a stream of bubbles rising from where he had been. I wondered if he had retreated to the lodge when I felt a gentle nudge below my knee, then a series of soft taps travelling all the way up my bare leg. The gentle underwater nudgings reminded me of the nibbling of curious minnows, but the beaver's nose, as he explored something new, did not give the sometimes painful nips that minnows give. One by one, the other young beavers came out and approached me warily, lifting their noses to sniff as they came. With their small black hands clutched against their chests, they teetered on the surface and now and then gave a fishlike flirt with their tails which propelled them nearer. Gradually they became bolder,

diving and nudging me with tickling noses. This alter-
nated with sudden spells of timidity when they rushed
off. But it was like children playing goblins—a game at
the same time self-protective but exhilarating. In the
end, they all clustered about me and I petted them."

Five-fifteen in the morning is Mrs. Buyukmihci's usual
rising hour. The habit began rather early in her life,
which started in the northern New York town of Lor-
raine. Her father, Edmund J. Sawyer, was a naturalist
and bird artist, whose love of nature and some of his
drawing ability, too, passed to his daughter. Many is-
sues of *The Beaver Defenders*, as well as this book, are
enlivened by her art. Explaining why she gets up so
early, Mrs. Buyukmihci says, "I feel the day is wasted
unless I'm up before the sun rises; it's important to me
to see earth's star ascend and night turn into day." The
habit got her into trouble with the president of Atlantic
Union College, a small Seventh Day Adventist school in
South Lancaster, Massachusetts, where she had matric-
ulated. The president saw no reason for a lone girl to
be wandering the college grounds in the pre-dawn dimness. However, her reason for leaving the institution
was not official disapproval of this practice but a short-
age of money. She went from there to Cornell University as an employee and worked as a sketcher of vertebrates in the nature-study department. In Ithaca she
met her future husband, an engineering student. They
were married in 1946.

Mrs. Buyukmihci's enthusiasm for an increased
beaver population is not shared by all the people on
whom the growing population impinges. Road maintenance men are apt to get grumpy when beaver dams
in viaducts cause road floodings. Farmers, too, are net-
tled when water backed up by beaver dams inundates

low-lying acreage. And city folks, as well, have been known to join the anti-beaver group; the ponds that beavers create on summer properties can attract shoals of frogs whose nocturnal thrummings often make sleep by the vacationing owners a difficult matter. However, Mrs. Buyukmihci answers all such complaints by saying that beavers are far more beneficial than harmful. "Beavers," she asserts, "are important water conservationists and potent agents of flood protection. On a stream with beaver ponds, water is spread out. Under heavy downpours, it simply spreads out more and is delayed in reaching and flooding the areas downstream. Where timber fires start in beaver country, the streams' flowages are often the most important, sometimes the only, source of water for portable pumps and hoses. The work of the beavers helps other wildlife species, too, particularly fish and waterfowl, and it is especially important in maintaining a stable water table and preventing needless erosion. Loren Eiseley, the naturalist, puts it well when, in a poem to the beaver, he writes, 'He knew something, kept in his own way a continent from sliding into the sea.'"

Mrs. Buyukmihci and I met at her New Jersey home during the beginning of the Beaver Moon, the full moon of November, so named long ago by the American Indians, because then the beavers' fur, from which they made robes, was at its prime. I pulled up before the renovated cabin, now a five-room house, a front room of which Mrs. Buyukmihci uses as her studio. There she writes, draws, and develops film that she has taken of beavers. Her literary production, besides the monthly newsletter, includes two books on beavers and articles for such publications as *The Ford Times*. Any spare funds that she and her husband acquire go to advance the cause of the beaver, the highest priority of which at the moment is to find financing to buy some adjoining land bearing buildings that would make an ideal humane education center. Educating children and adults to the good points of the beaver, as well as those of other wild creatures, is, Mrs. Buyukmihci now feels after years of struggle, the best hope for achieving significant protection for beaver and all other threatened wildlife species.

As twilight approached, Mrs. Buyukmihci and I went out to call on some beavers. We were both warmly dressed against the autumn chill. Mrs. Buyukmihci carried a heavy-duty flashlight and I a large kitchen pan of peeled and quartered apples that she had prepared, tidbits much appreciated, I was told, by beavers. Whiskers and Greenbriar were elsewhere these days, and the beaver family we hoped to see consisted of Lenape, a male; his mate, October; Sprite, a yearling; and P.S., a kit, who received his odd appellation because he seemed to be an afterthought, a singleton baby born in late summer.

The sky was sodden gray with a soft pink band in the west as we walked along a path under leafless gums and maples in the refuge, speckled here and there with a few green conifer clumps. After about five minutes, we reached the start of a quarter of a mile of rather rickety, homemade boardwalk laid over swamp water dotted with dead-grass tussocks. At its end we came to a small open slope on a stream above a beaver dam. Mrs. Buyukmihci and I sat down there, and she began to call softly, "Here beaver, beaver, beaver. Here beaver." We did not see Lenape, October, or P.S. that evening, and Mrs. Buyukmihci was especially disappointed by P.S.'s absence. "He would have surely said a few words to us," she told me. But Sprite was very much on the scene. He appeared after several minutes

Lenape feeding.

of Mrs. Buyukmihci's calling. He seemed quite relaxed in her presence, but somewhat uncertain about mine. In fact, at the start he was notably standoffish. He remained in the water about six feet distant, watching me carefully with his large, intelligent eyes and wiggling his nose undisguisedly in my direction. Instead of coming up at once to Mrs. Buyukmihci for hand-feeding and patting, he stayed his distance and was coaxed to take food only after Mrs. Buyukmihci had speared an apple quarter on a long stick and thrust it out over the water to him. He removed the apply piece with his adept front paws, took it to the other side of the stream, climbed out and started to eat it with quick nibbles of his incisors, a task he obviously relished. His teeth made crunching noises as he bit through the fruit. From his look out of water, I would say that he weighed something over twenty pounds, relating his size to that of my thirty-pound Corgi. He was quick and decisive in his movements, and had a personality with which I, at any rate, was quite empathic, despite whatever reservations he may have had at first about mine. Soon he came back for more apple. Before long he was feeding from Mrs. Buyukmihci's hand and, in due course, from mine. It was hunting season, and during our interlude on the bank the sound of guns from time to time came from the area outside the refuge. Sprite paid no attention to these, but then a light plane droned overhead and the sound of its passage coincided with that of a gun. Instantly Sprite upended and dove. It was an inordinately quick and graceful motion, so skilled that it left scarcely a ripple. A line of little silver spheres marked his underwater wake. "The two unnatural sounds coming together alarmed him," Mrs. Buyukmihci explained. "He could have taken either alone, but the pair were too much for him. I'll try to get him back." She called and soon Sprite returned, bringing his appetite with him. It was dark when the pan at last was empty. "Goodnight, Sprite," Mrs. Buyukmihci said. We needed the flashlight going back. Night mists were rising from the swamp.

11

Virgin Forest

Some of the individual trees standing in Central Park were there at least a century and a quarter ago when the question of a large park for the growing metropolis on the Hudson River was under general discussion. But the last piece of virgin forest remaining in New York City stands in the Bronx in the northern part of the grounds of the New York Botanical Garden. It lies along both banks of the Bronx River, but principally on the western slope of the valley, through which the river runs from north to south, rising up the valley's heights till it spills over the crest of a rocky ridge. The forest occupies some forty of the 230 acres to be found in the Garden, extending on the west side of the river from the institution's northern boundary southward a matter of 2,000 feet to a point nearly opposite the Lorillard snuff mill on the eastern bank. The forest's greatest width, some 900 feet, is at a location about 700 feet above a waterfall in the river. The trees are a mixture of hardwoods and hemlocks, the latter being notable as the most southerly stand of any number to be met so close to the Atlantic seaboard. William E. Dodge, one of the original incorporators of the Botanical Garden, called the forest "the most precious natural possession of the City of New York."

History records no ax or saw ever being used in it. Supposedly, it has stood as it now stands since Indians were the inhabitants of our continent. The trees of the forest have grown, matured, died, and been replaced by others without interruption over the centuries, so far as is known. Certainly the Lorillard family, which purchased fifty acres along the Bronx River in 1792, later acquiring much additional land, permitted no lumbering there. The family bought the property for the grist mill it contained but shortly thereafter abandoned this building and in about 1800 constructed a bit higher up the river, the handsome stone snuff mill that the Garden now uses as a restaurant. The mills were for grinding tobacco that the Lorillards, long lucratively engaged in the business, dispensed as snuff to devotees of the then fashionable habit through a store they maintained in Manhattan.

In 1884 the City of New York purchased 661 acres of the Lorillards' Bronx property, including the snuff mill and the land on which the forest stands. The city transferred the acquisition to the Parks Department, which, in turn, gave 400 acres with the mill and the forest to the Garden, established a few years later. Over the years, principally through demands by the city for roadways, this has dwindled to the present 230 acres.

Recently, I telephoned Dr. Howard S. Irwin, the Garden's director, and asked whether, with a guide who was knowledgeable in botany, I could take a walk through the reaches of the forest. Its primal character links it to a bygone era when the clear waters of the five boroughs were crammed with fish, and their surfaces crowned with soaring trees under which game animals and the original inhabitants wandered. I was curious to see how something so closely related to that tranquil past has reacted to today's environment with its burgeoning population and its complicated technology. For forests are communities of living things. Thus a virgin forest, which foresters prefer to call mature or climactic, is rigidly subject to the interconnected workings of ecology. These, sometimes in a period considerably less than the life expectancy of the ruling trees, can change the character of a virgin forest by altering the numbers and kinds of the species within it. Lightning-induced fires and intervention by men constitute powerful threats to the permanence of the forest community.

Dr. Irwin suggested that if I come to the Museum, the main administration building of the Garden, Larry Pardue, the plant information officer, would be glad to accompany me through the forest. Subsequently, at the Museum I met Mr. Pardue, a twenty-five-year old graduate of the University of Southern Florida, with a master's degree in botany and a record of five years' work at the Garden. For our walk he also brought along Mrs. Doris M. Stone, a graduate some years back of Oxford University, who is resource teacher in botany and horticulture in the Garden and a member of its teaching training program, a project designed for the benefit of faculty members of the city's schools.

We left the Museum, walking along a paved auto

road for several hundred feet until we moved onto a graveled highway that led up a slope to the ridge over which the forest spills. A Garden safari truck passed us on the road, and Pardue said it was going on patrol duty in the forest. "More than fifty years ago," he continued, "when the number of people walking in the forest had increased to such an extent that channeling the traffic was thought desirable, a series of fairly wide trails, passable by auto, was laid out, some lined with iron railings. We still request the public to use the trails, but we don't enforce it. Most people today, I'm afraid, just walk where they want. Naturally, with the large number visiting the Garden and using the forest these days a periodic check of the woods on our part is necessary."

A few minutes after starting our climb, we passed a large, unusual-looking tree, whose bark hung in great strips from the trunk, making one think of a beggar clad in tatters. "A shagbark hickory," Pardue said. "Its wood is hard, heavy, tough, strong, and elastic. Things like golf clubs, baseball bats, and tool handles are made from it." We were beginning to move now under fairly tall trees as we continued to mount the slope, and Pardue took the occasion to point out some of the small trees and shrubs below them. He called this the understory. It is woody vegetation that grows in the light falling through spaces in the forest or through the leaves of the trees above it. He noted arrowwood, a viburnum, a sizable shrub whose tough, pliant shoots were once used for arrows, as well as several other viburnums, members of a family of shrubs and small trees very common in eastern North America; young beeches and sugar maples; the spice bush, an aromatic plant whose powdered berries are sometimes a substitute for all-spice; cherry birch, capable of producing oil of wintergreen; and the Hercules Club, whose leaves are the largest of any North American tree—they can reach almost four feet in length and two in width—a factor that made this odd little specimen a favorite for lawn decoration of spacious homes in Victorian times, along with cast-iron deer or dogs. Also catching Pardue's eye was pokeweed, a coarse perennial with dark purple, juicy berries that, uncooked, are emetic and purgative. "But cooking removes these qualities," he said. "In the Middle West housewives make pies of them."

We now had left the graveled roadway and were walking under the trees along a footpath beside which we shortly came upon the fallen trunk of a great red oak. I asked Pardue whether it would be left on the ground as a nurse log, its elements, as decay progressed, returning to the soil to nourish neighboring plants. "That's not for me to say," he replied, but the tone of his voice indicated quite clearly that he hoped it would. "The tree," he added, "fell last year in a storm. Apparently it had been struck by lightning years ago and decay entered through the wound destroying the heartwood. We didn't know the oak was hollow until it fell."

Heartwood lies at the interior of the trunk. In the case of a mature tree, it occupies most of it, displaying the majority of the annual growth rings that tell the tree's age. Heartwood is dead wood, serving the tree only as support. It no longer conducts water up to the leaves. Thus a tree can go on living and growing without its heartwood. But it is more likely to fall or break if it is hollow. Heartwood, which in a healthy tree is solid and undiseased, is the part most prized for lumber. Heartwood, too, of course, is also present in the branches, roots, and larger twigs, only the very newest growth being without it.

Outside the heartwood is the sapwood, generally of a lighter color in most trees. It constitutes most of the recently produced annual growth rings. Sapwood is essential to the life of the tree and thus is present in all its woody parts. Sapwood carries water and dissolved minerals gathered by the root hairs and transmits them through ducts along the larger roots and up the trunk, branches, and twigs to the leaves, which use them in producing food. Surrounding the sapwood is the vital vascular cambium tissue, a very thin cylindrical sheath usually only several cells thick, that entirely envelops the tree's woody structure from the crown's highest tip to the outermost part of the root system. The cambium layer is the growing tissue. It causes increase in girth of stems and roots. During the growing season its cells are constantly reproducing, not only renewing itself but also forming other types of cells. Those on the inside become the newest annual growth ring; those on the outside form phloem tissue, which carries food—sugar, amino acids, and so forth—from the leaves to all parts of the plant. Growth is not even-paced during the spring and summer growing season. Most of it takes place in the spring, in some trees almost entirely during the first several weeks. Trees increase in length only in the tips of the crown and roots, where, of course, there are also actively dividing cells. The growth in the trunk is entirely in girth. Initials, for example, carved in one are found to be exactly at the same height, should the carver return to the spot ten or even fifty years later. Animals cease their growth at maturity; trees, however, grow until they die.

The phloem tissue at the inside of the bark is very thin. In pine trees, for example, it is slick and white. In all trees it is composed mostly of two kinds of slender channels, one vertical, the sieve tubes, and the other horizontal, the vascular rays. The sieve tubes carry the food manufactured by the leaves downward; the vascular rays carry it laterally. Thus every part of the tree is nourished. Very young growth is covered by the epidermis. Often it is so thin that it has a greenish tinge, caused by the chlorophyll of the cortex, a green tissue lying just outside the phloem tissue. Usually, only the leaves have chlorophyll but there is also some present in the young stem. As the bark ages, it contains the following strata, moving from the inside out: the phelloderm, a storage tissue, and the phellogen, sometimes called the cork cambium, the layers of cells that manufacture both the phelloderm and the cork, which laymen refer to as the bark. The cork, or the bark, the trunk's rugged cover, incidentally, has certain interesting properties. It possesses suberin, a waxy substance that stops the passage of water and gases, thus averting dehydration. Its cells also contain air, an excellent insulator against heat and cold, thus protecting the delicate cambium layer from temperature extremes. And, finally, the cork forms a protective coat against mechanical damage. When cuts or wounds penetrate the bark, the phellogen produces a healing layer, barring the fungi of decay.

Leaves, whether the needles of evergreens or those of the broad-leaved variety, manufacture the tree's food. Mainly this is a simple sugar called glucose, produced by the process of photosynthesis, whereby water from the roots, carbon dioxide from the air, and solar energy absorbed by the green chlorophyll combine to form the sugar. The many steps, all taking place in microseconds, are still largely unclarified. But a much simplified description of what happens is that light energy splits water molecules, liberating oxygen, which is returned to the environment. The hydrogen component of the water molecules, in a very complicated series of steps, joins with the carbon dioxide to produce the glucose

The carbon dioxide taken in from the atmosphere and the oxygen returned to it pass through tiny openings, called stomates, on the undersides of the leaves. Their number is prodigious, a maple leaf possessing more than 100,000 within a square inch. Although it might appear that broad-leaved trees would have considerably more leaf surface than evergreens, the reverse as a rule is true, due to the profusion of needles. A pair of semicircular guard cells on either side of the pore open and close the stomate, their action being regulated by a complex sequence of events. Only 1 percent, or less, of sunlight falling on a leaf is used in food production, the rest of the energy being lost or reflected back into space. A tree absorbs a surprising amount of water from the ground. A large apple tree was found to take in four gallons an hour, only a very small part of which was used in food production, the rest being transpired as vapor.

The tree's metabolism converts most of the food into cellulose, of which wood is largely composed. The chemical composition of cellulose is $C_6H_{10}O_5$, but the number of these units in the cellulose, which is invariably a macromolecule, runs into the hundreds of thousands—an example of natural polymer chemistry. The trace minerals dissolved in the water channelled aloft by the roots and used in the tree's physiology in various complex ways, is recoverable as ash when a log is burned. In the flames carbon atoms of the cellulose combine with oxygen atoms from the air, going up the chimney as carbon dioxide. They return to the carbon-dioxide sink in the atmosphere to be used ultimately once again in photosynthesis. Cellulose's hydrogen and oxygen follow the same route, returning to the atmosphere as molecules of water vapor. Of what was once a log, only the trace minerals remain on the hearth in the form of ash.

A leaf's structure is divided into three principal parts. Covering both sides is the epidermis, a single-celled layer under a waxy film called the cuticle, which limits evaporation. Between the upper and lower epidermis is the mesophyll. This has the apparatus for producing food, primarily the chloroplasts, astonishingly numerous small green discs possessing the substance chlorophyll, which absorbs the energy for photosynthesis. Of chloroplasts the average leaf possesses a quantity even greater than that of its abundant stomates, a square inch holding a quarter of a billion or more chloroplasts. Like the rest of the tree, the leaf has two conducting systems, one for bringing in the raw material for food and the other for distributing the finished product to all parts of the organism. This conductive tissue is the third part of the leaf—the vascular bundles or veins. Woody xylem cells form the tubes bringing in minerals and water, and they are strong enough to act as ribs, supporting the structure of the leaf. Thin-walled phloem cells form the pipes carrying the food made by the mesophyll out of it to the rest of the tree. The vascular bundles are arranged so that every part of the mesophyll is no more than a cell length or two distant from a segment of the vascular bundles.

A tree's root system in the temperate zone, which, of course, is where the virgin forest stands, may be one of two kinds, either what is called a fibrous root system possessed by such trees as hemlocks, elms, birch, and beech or a taproot system found in oaks, walnuts, and hickories. The generally held belief that a tree's root system spreads out only as far as the periphery of its crown is incorrect. In both types of systems it reaches out considerably farther. The fibrous root system, though extensive, is shallow. Accordingly, its owners may suffer blowdowns in storms that leave oaks and other tap-rooted trees, whose central primary may descend to a depth of thirty feet, still standing upright and unharmed. Besides the duty of anchoring a tree to the ground, the root system has the important task of serving as storehouse for food during the tree's cold-induced period of dormancy, not to mention the system's third important job, that of absorbing water and minerals for the manufacture of food.

One of the marvels of the roots is their extent, particularly the fine root hairs that do most of the absorption. Roots, in a pattern that is well known, branch and rebranch profusely until at the very ends are to be found tips with a minute, protective cap like a shield back of which the tissue pushes and the roots grow outward, forcing their way around or through hard obstacles. Back of the cap for only an inch or so are the short-lived, almost microscopically fine root hairs that take in the vital water and dissolved minerals from the ground. They can locate water, quantities of it, when to unaided human eyes the soil seems utterly arid.

Botanists have yet to count the number and area of the roots of a large tree. But a study has been made of the roots of rye, a grass. It was found that a single plant, four months old, had put out 378 miles of roots, with more than 14 billion root hairs, whose surface was in excess of 4,000 square feet. This considerably surpasses the area of a regulation tennis court. The whole was contained within only two cubic feet of soil.

Another feature of the roots of many forest trees is the white strands of fungus that collect around them. The strands either penetrate the roots, or more usually in forest trees, form investing sheaths, causing them to branch into clublike structures. These composite organs of root and fungus are called mycorhizae. The fungus does indeed take its food from the roots, but the relationship has been found to be beneficial to the host. The fungus's action in making the roots produce mycorhizae increases the amount of water and minerals that they can take up, partially by increasing the surface area of the roots. This subterranean symbiosis is important in the lives of many trees; in fact, it is vital to their existence on soils deficient in mineral salts.

We left the fallen red oak and continued our walk, passing under or alongside a number of mature trees. "That tulip tree is 125 feet tall," said Pardue, pointing it out, "and more than 200 years old." The tulip is the tallest hardwood tree in eastern North America. Its trunk runs erect—tall and branchless—for many feet. As one naturalist put it, it always looks young no matter what its age. The woods we travelled now were fairly open, lacking an appreciable understory, and the trees were somewhat widely spaced. "That white oak," said Pardue, indicating a squat, heavy, gnarled tree, "is even older than the tulip. It grows much more slowly. It is, I suspect, one of the oldest trees in the forest." Taking a tape measure from my pocket, I found the diameter breast-high of its ponderous trunk to be three and a half feet. "That beech over there," said Pardue, calling our attention to a robust tree with beautiful smooth gray bark, "is the oldest of its species I know of here." Its small, triangular-shaped nuts are highly regarded by forest birds and animals. The nuts have a mealy taste, presumably duplicated in beechnut chewing gum. The tree's name comes from the Anglo-Saxon word *bece*, meaning book, because runic tablets were made from slabs of its hard, fine-grained wood. The ground under the hemlock trees we passed was spongy with fallen needles. "Evergreens like other trees do lose their leaves," said Pardue. "But not annually. A portion of the hemlock's leaves, for example, are shed each season and renewed."

Pardue now asked us to note the thick foliage under which we were passing; then he led us to an open space in the forest caused by a huge, loaf-shaped rock rising out of the ground. The rocky extrusion was Fordham gneiss, an enormous, coarse-grained outcropping with imperfect folds alternating in light and dark bands. It represented part of the oldest of the three bedrock systems underlying New York City, all of which were laid down in seas of the early Paleozoic era some 400 million years ago and later heavily metamorphosed. The two others are Inwood marble and Manhattan schist, the latter being the youngest of the three.

From atop the Fordham gneiss we had a good view of the crowns of the trees we had just passed under. The tops of several hemlocks and an oak were bare above their verdant lower branches. "Aerial pollution is a suspect factor here," said Pardue, "although we can't be certain." He went on to say that sometimes when the wind blew from the heavily urbanized areas to the south or southwest the atmosphere in the Garden would become a light blue-gray, carrying with it an odor of petroleum fuel, sulphur, or both. He remarked that his reaction then was one of slight nausea. "It makes my eyes prickle," said Mrs. Stone.

The big rock lay near the crest of the ridge up which we had been walking and we left it to travel diagonally down the slope of the other side toward the snuff mill to the south. We sometimes walked over the forest floor and sometimes used narrow paths made, Pardue said, by walkers in the woods, a number of whom are dedicated birders. From time to time in the distance

among the trees we could see solitary figures, couples
or groups, the most striking of which was a Spanish-
speaking family of five by whom we passed quite close,
parents and children clad in serapes and seeming to
have much Indian blood.

"Hi, you guys! Clear out of there," suddenly called
Pardue. He was yelling at two fairly large dogs, running
free, that had just appeared in front of us. The animals
took the hint and quickly disappeared. "Chasing squirrels, probably," said Pardue. He added that besides squirrels there were chipmunks, rabbits, pheasants, and
foxes in the forest. As we descended, Pardue showed
us an outsized gall on the trunk of a distant red oak. Galls
are swellings produced in the tissue of plants by vegetable or animal organisms, sometimes harmful, sometimes not. The growth was literally as large as an ele-
phant's head. "That's the biggest gall we have in the
Garden. But the tree, despite it, seems to be doing
well," he said.

We then came to an area of bottom land beside
the Bronx River with the snuff mill in sight some 300
yards away on the other side of the stream. Not far
away we could hear the waterfall gurgling. Sunlight
came through the leaves dappling the ground around us.
Some rotting logs lay on it, and there was other good
detritus in the form of fallen branches and leaves. Fungi
sprouted up from the soil, among them clumps of tiny-
gilled, gold-topped mushrooms. "There are more mature trees right around us here than in any other portion of the Garden," said Pardue. A number of hemlocks
were visible, but most of what we saw were deciduous
trees. "That sweet gum there," said Mrs. Stone,
designating a specimen better than 100 feet high, "is
the tallest I've ever seen." (The species, sometimes
called liquidamber, produces a fragrant gum. Monte-

zuma, during a meeting with Cortez, mixed it with tobacco and smoked the combination in a pipe, according to an observer of the scene.) From where we stood, we could see one of the wide paths, running along the Bronx River, carefully laid out for public use during the Garden's early history. The sturdy iron railings beside it were rusted and often twisted and broken by years of vandalism. Paths branched randomly away from it.

"There are more mature trees right around here than any place I know of in southern New York."

In a metropolis today a virgin forest unavoidably differs from one, say, surrounding a still blue lake in a remote section of Minnesota. For one thing, of course, there is the city's atmospheric pollution, both automotive and industrial. But more than that there is the influx of people, a constant heavy traffic that tramples

seedlings and packs down the soil, thereby increasing runoff and erosion, conditions that are harmful to a natural forest state; in addition, there is always some vandalism involving the trunks and branches of the trees themselves. "Forest protection, to the extent possible, is, of course, a Garden aim," said Pardue. "In that part of the forest, for example, that approaches the snuff mill, where traffic is less, forest conditions are much more normal. Although it is a small area, there are several hemlock seedlings growing there. In the entire rest of the forest, I believe there are only two or three. To achieve more natural conditions, we have actually been thinking of protecting the forest floor by building boardwalks over the footpaths and directing pedestrian traffic to the boardwalk by means of a perimeter fence. Using boardwalks, which could be moved from one part of the forest to another every few years, could allow the public to continue to enjoy walking through the forest, yet still give the hemlock seedlings, and others, a chance to take hold."

At the time when the Botanical Garden took over the site the forest, in fact, was known as the Hemlock Forest. Dr. N. L. Britton, writing in the *Transactions of the Bronx Society of Arts and Sciences* in 1906 describes the trees as predominantly hemlock with an intermingling of beech, hickory, oaks, tulip, and other deciduous species. The forest then was dark and funereal rather than fairly open as at present. Twenty years later, in an article in the *Journal of the New York Botanical Garden*, it was stated that a 1923 count of hemlocks in the forest showed 3,600 large and small trees, seedlings not included. Today there is only a tiny fraction of that amount.

In 1923, of course, traffic through the forest was comparatively minimal. The city then had 2 million

fewer people and, more important, their require-
ments for energy, with its attendant aerial pollution,
were far less than now. Thus the city's sole remaining
virgin forest, which never experienced saw or ax, has,
within a span of half a century, changed completely in
character from a dense hemlock forest to an open one,
primarily of deciduous trees, a turn evidently brought
about by increased human use and perhaps by atmospheric pollution as well. Furthermore, the outlook for
its future is not bright. A healthy forest is one that is re-
generating. Vigorous young saplings and seedlings
should be evident. This, alas, is not the case with the
New York Botanical Garden's virgin forest.

12

The Park's Microscopic Soil Life

More than 12 million people use Central Park each year, making it the most heavily visited park in the United States. However, it is virtually certain that practically none of them ever thinks of the life that lies within the earth beside the paths or under the grass over which they stroll. Yet a teeming cosmos inhabits these places; its numbers can fog the mind. In fact, the quantity of living things that may dwell in the top three inches of a square foot of Central Park soil can by many times exceed the entire human population of our planet. These creatures, which include bacteria, fungi, and protozoa, are known to deviate very exactly to reflect the environment, their multitudinous species and numbers changing according to such factors as the season, temperature, and moisture and makeup of the soil. Thus microorganisms from a Kansas prairie would differ from those below the needles of a New England pine forest. Even such contiguous tracts as adjacent suburban backyards, one tree-shaded, the other not, would be found to vary in microorganisms were the soil to be carefully screened.

In an effort to see just what might be present in those earthy lairs in the Park, I went to it one early-winter morning and collected five samples of soil. The first I took from a rather beaten tract beside a path on Pilgrim Hill not far from the park's entrance on Fifth Avenue at Seventy-second Street. The next came from loose, leaf-covered soil under the Fifth Avenue wall due east of Conservatory Lake and the Krebs Memorial Boathouse; this was soil much like the type one would find on a forest floor outside the reaches of the city, except that near my sample was an empty pint wine bottle and the weathered remains of a Cracker Jack box. The third specimen came from a meadow on Cedar Hill, the popular dog-exercising slope, and the fourth was dug from under the limbs of a young Norway maple in the heavily wooded Ramble. All had the characteristic dark look of topsoil. For the last example I wanted something from lower down. So I went farther west in the Park, not far from the Delacorte Outdoor Theater, where a municipal water tunnel was being dug. From the excavated material I took a portion of lighter-colored dirt that a workman told me had come some days before from about five feet down. The small trowel I used in each case took enough earth to half fill five hinged plastic Woolworth soap dishes whose tops bore labels reading from 1 to 5.

I took the samples to the Brown Building of New York University on the northeast corner of Washington Square Park and left them by prearrangement at the office of Dr. Gunther Stotzky, the head of N. Y. U.'s Department of Biology. Dr. Stotzky, I had been told by people at the American Museum of Natural History, was quite knowledgeable about soil organisms, and he had earlier agreed over the telephone to have a look at what I might bring him. Stotzky, a man in his early forties with a close-cropped beard and just a trace of the academic administrator's harried manner, told me to come back in three days after he and two of his women graduate students, Dr. Rafia Mehdi and Mrs. Kathy Hartman, had had a chance to do some research and also to cultivate in petri dishes for identification some of the strains of fungi that might be present.

On my return at the appointed time, Dr. Stotzky received me in his office. His first question was where in the Park the samples had come from. When I told him, he said, "That's very interesting. The first two samples of topsoil, those from the path on Pilgrim Hill and from the loose soil lying under the Fifth Avenue wall, had in each case about the same population of bacteria, the first with 15 million bacteria to the gram of soil and the second with a figure of over 13 million. The second, however, with its looser soil structure, possessed almost twice the amount of water held by the first. Footsteps of park users evidently had somewhat compressed the first sample's soil, eliminating part of the water content by forcing it downward. The first sample contained 8.7 percent water per gram; the second had 13.6 percent water. This element is vitally necessary to soil creatures. In fact, all underground life may be said to exist in a watery world, a thought that offhand might seem quite odd to the man in the street. Yet, nevertheless, it's true.

"The phenomenon of compression, which takes place to some degree wherever walkers wander over the Park's natural surface, also caused a difference in the two samples of the quantity of fungi found. Fungi are obligate aerobes. That is, they need the oxygen found in the air to live, and they thrive best where it is plentiful. Therefore, where footsteps pack down the soil, lessening the underground spaces where air can gather, the fungi population is decreased. The first sample contains only 130,000 fungi per gram while the second has almost half a million.

"The fourth topsoil sample," Stotzky went on, "the one from under the young maple tree in the Ramble, has, as you might expect in the spongy soil under its leaf litter, a high moisture content, a matter of 12.4 percent per gram. However, its bacteria and fungi count are surprisingly low, only 4 million bacteria and 124,000 fungi per gram being found. A substance secreted by the roots and leaves of the maple may have caused this low life density. Further research, however, would be necessary to establish this.

"Sample Number Five, rather stony and coarse, which is the only deep-soil specimen, came from about five feet down and was lying at the surface for a while. Its water content was 10 percent, and the bacteria count was about as high as those of the first two samples, a circumstance that probably resulted from bacteria in the air, where they are always present in large numbers, infiltrating the sample as it lay at the surface. However, the fungi at 55,000 per gram were lower than in any sample tested. This, of course, was to be anticipated. The deeper the soil, the fewer the fungi, due to a relative absence of oxygen. The sample evidently had not been lying at the surface long enough to become an ordinary topsoil specimen. On the third sample, the one taken from the meadow on Cedar Hill, we did not make a population count. It seemed composed mostly of grass and roots."

The pH reading of all, Stotzky said, was 4.5. This scale denotes the acidity or alkalinity of material, on which pH 7 indicates neutrality. Thus the samples were distinctly acid. This would have been predictable, Stotzky added. New York City has large quantities of sulphuric acid in the air from combustion fumes from chimneys. The rain precipitates this as sulphuric acid.

A gram of soil can be considered as a cube that is roughly two-fifths of an inch on a side. Thus the top three inches of a square foot of earth would contain 1,080 grams. Extrapolating, for instance, the statistics from Sample Two to an area of this size, one finds that it would have 14,256,000,000 bacteria and 515,160,000 fungi, or a total of nearly 15 billion living things. This is a number that is more than four times greater than the human population of the earth.

Nor does that, by any means, exhaust the forms of life inhabiting the material that I had gathered. Other minute organisms that Stotzky and his students had found under the microscope from the samples received were numerous algae and protozoans. These are, respectively, minuscule plants and animals. Usually, they dwell in fresh and salt water under the open sky, but these existed within the water particles of the soil. "Doubtless, too," Stotzky said, "many other forms of life typical of the temperate-zone soil environment are also present, including mites, pseudoscorpions, slime molds, nematodes, springtails, and

various insect larvae." In fact, in collecting Sample
Two, I had come across several larvae which I had not
put in the soap dish but had returned to the soil. The
creatures that Stotzky had mentioned as likely proba-
bilities to be found in the samples were all members
of the animal kingdom, in contrast to the bacteria and
fungi, which are plants—all, that is, with the exception
of the slime molds, about which scientists are still of
two minds. Some call them animals; some call them
plants.

In addition to these very small beings, all below
the level of normal visibility or reaching barely above it,
the Central Park soil, either in the vicinity where I
had collected the samples, or elsewhere, possesses
larger and better-known underground denizens. Earthworms, wireworms, millipedes, ants, and various
beetles are among those that tunnel diligently under
the surface. While their number is insignificant compared with that of the microorganisms, they create
relatively enormous passageways in the soil. These
provide wide conduits for the entry of air and water,
thus substantially increasing the pace at which life can
be carried on below. Indeed, one investigator has computed that the biota of an acre of topsoil gives off as
much energy as would be produced by 10,000 human
beings living and working atop the area (a circumstance that would require the unfortunate bipeds,
however, to be confined to a Lebensraum barely two
feet square). The changing seasons, of course, vary the
number of the soil organisms, Stotzky said. Normally
they peak in spring and autumn, declining in summer
and winter. The causes of decline are summer's customary dryness and winter's customary chill. However,
when a wet summer occurs or a winter with a cold-
resistant ground cover of snow, the declines lessen.

The main role of soil bacteria and fungi anywhere on earth is to break down into simple, usable materials the litter that the galaxy of living things deposits each year on the surface of the earth. In addition to the lifeless leaves of trees, shrubs, and grass, the debris includes twigs, branches, flowers, fruit, animal excrement, and animal remains and, in the case of Central Park, gum wrappers and so forth. The bacteria and fungi, many endowed with life spans of only a matter of minutes or hours, attack this rubbish sturdily, breaking up man's refuse in the park as readily as nature's there and elsewhere. Their powers in this respect are notable. Scientists in experiments have fed them substances not found in nature, and these have halted them not at all. Their ability to decompose is one of the most important functions that living things perform anywhere. Carbon, nitrogen, and other elements essential to the growth of plants emerge from their labors in a steady stream, an absolutely imperative procedure in life's continuance, because the supply of these critical elements is limited in nature. Were they not being continuously unlocked from dead materials that possess them, all plant life on earth and all animal life there, too (since it depends on the former) would soon hesitate, stumble, and drag to a halt. For example, the supply of available carbon in the earth's biosphere would vanish completely in fifteen years without the process of recycling, it is estimated. Only consider for a moment a forest floor choked with the debris of several years lying like so much inert metal on the surface with all the young plants and seedlings unable to break through. Then the need for recycling becomes only too crystal clear.

Another important by-product of bacterial decomposition of rubbish, particularly dead leaves, may be leaf dust. These tiny remnants of decomposition can be carried by atmospheric currents high into the air. Meteorologists are now studying the possibility that this powdery stuff contributes greatly to the formation of cloud-borne ice particles, a necessary preliminary to all kinds of precipitation. If, as is now thought, the ice particles must form in supercooled clouds before precipitation starts, the particles would require cores to condense around, and scientists are now investigating whether many of these are not bits of leaf dust, produced by soil bacteria. Thus these tiny creatures not only play a part in the recycling of vital elements but may also be responsible to a considerable degree in bringing water in all its forms down from the skies to reinvigorate the earth.

Photosynthesis is the plant activity probably best known to the layman. In it the plant takes carbon dioxide from the air, minerals in watery solution from the earth, and radiant energy from the sun; these it turns into sugars, which it uses for energy and the production of body components, and into oxygen and water, which it expels through the pores in its leaves. Some photosynthesis by algae and bacteria occurs, too, in the soil environment, Stotzky said, but it is restricted to the surface portion. Naturally, it is at its greatest where the sunlight can fall directly atop the loose material lying on the ground, and it lessens in the shadow of the layers farther down. The energy produced by the process is used in litter dissolution. Photosynthesis is also possible in the top few millimeters of bare ground, but below that it stops. There the zone of eternal night begins.

In this domain of everlasting dark, decomposition proceeds quite differently. Two very broad types of bacteria are there, Stotzky said: autotrophs and heterotrophs. The autotrophs exist on basic chemical elements such as iron, nitrogen, and sulphur, turning them into more complex substances suitable for plants. Among them are some of the organisms that can fix nitrogen, the stubbornly inert element that comprises nearly four-fifths of our atmosphere. Once they have transformed it into a nitrate, the nitrogen atoms can then be used practically indefinitely thereafter by plants through the recycling process. The more numerous heterotrophs live on preformed carbon compounds (that is, matter that was once alive), keeping for their own tiny bodies only a minute fraction of what they decompose. Among their numbers are the *Actinomycetes*, a contributor to virtually everyone's memory bank. On a fresh spring morning in Central Park the bouquet from a gardener's spadeful of freshly turned earth there (or elsewhere) is simply the odor of *Actinomycetes*.

The multifarious bacteria, consisting of hundreds of species, are almost the smallest inhabitants of the soil cosmos, usually measuring merely from one to five microns, or from 1/25,000 to 1/5,000 inch in length. Perhaps the only smaller thing may be one of their predators, a kind of virus called a bacteriophage. These, along with many larger organisms, do their best to consume as many bacteria as possible, undoubtedly a good thing all around, for bacteria, which propagate by fission or by dividing their body in two, are enormously prolific. A single individual, for example, of a variety that can do this every twenty minutes has the potential to produce in a couple of days offspring that would many times outweigh the earth.

The second large group of soil organisms, the fungi, are all heterotrophs. While toadstools and mushrooms are two well-known examples of the group, the main decomposers among the fungi are scores of kinds of sickly looking plants whose bodies are composed of strands, or nets, of often whitish or grayish fibers, sometimes so thickly meshed that they hold tightly together large quantities of soil particles. The strands, called mycelia, have many cells along them, each of which can, and often does, branch out to start a strand of its own, thus accounting for the astonishing tangle that can result. Fungi are found from the top to bottom of the soil environment, those kinds that can digest sugar being especially numerous at the top among the fresh-fallen leaves with their high sugar content, while lower down other varieties consume the cellulose and lignin of the older, more battered leaf fragments and join the heterotrophic bacteria in breaking up additional litter within the topsoil—the waste of all things that inhabit the environment—infertile insect eggs, dead larvae, cast skins, the excrement and corpses of the resident crew of micro- and macro-invertebrates and those of such vertebrates as the toad and the shrew, not to mention the dead and dying bodies of the bacteria and fungi themselves. (Toads and shrews still persist in the less-frequented parts of Central Park.) In the process, Stotzky said, much CO_2 is created, the ratio of this gas being ten to a hundred times higher in the soil's atmosphere than in the air above it. However, it does not remain for long below but continually leaks outside, where it becomes available for photosynthesis.

Topsoil is far from a solid material. Loose soil such as I gathered under the Fifth Avenue wall may have up to 50 percent empty space, and all soils have some. Topsoil is made of humus (decaying organic matter), mineral particles, and space. Were a man to be reduced to bacterium size and given a tiny light by which to see, he would enter a strange world, indeed, if he penetrated one inch down into the soil's region of eternal night. Before him the moist realm would stretch away into a misty, onreaching vista of huge caves to whose boulder sides would cling sheets of water inhabited by blue-green algae far larger than himself. Lakes filled with swimming protozoa would be there and monsters roaming on the shores in the shape of micro- and macro-animals, too diversified, horrendous, and threatening to be briefly described. It is a fantastic scene, perhaps one of the few sci-fi possibilities remaining to be used as a cinema setting.

On any boulder in Central Park the start of topsoil's story can be observed. Lichens cling to the bare surface, their brisk metabolic acids loosening the rock particles below. When the lichens die, their bodies and

A boulder shows the start of topsoil's story.

air-borne dust make a bed suitable for the mosses, the next step in the soil's formation. Slowly, very slowly, the process goes forward. Eons upon eons went into the manufacture of the soil lying at the boulder's foot, as into that lying elsewhere on our planet.

Roots are another highly important constituent of the soil. Those of trees, shrubs, and grass have the same structure—a four-phased pattern beginning with the enormously tough and powerful root cap, which is like a construction worker's hard hat pushing through the soil (and through clefts in rocks if need be), followed by the short length of the root that grows. Back of this are the massed, tiny root hairs imbibing nutrients in solution from the soil. These have only a brief life while the growing part moves forward to allow new hairs to form and seek fresh food. At the end is the fourth part, the old brown basal root. The root hairs drink in the thin film of moisture that surrounds the soil particles. This is constantly replaced in the soil through capillary attraction by water from farther down, a fact that permits one of the Park's large red oaks to consume as much as fifty gallons on a summer's day. When the roots, or portions of them, die, they, too, are instantly attacked and disintegrated by the soil organisms, their substance further enriching the soil. "In fact," said Stotzky, "if you wanted to make a simple generalization about *all* of the organisms that inhabit the soil, the generalization would be, 'They eat.'"

After a fifteen-minute chat, Stotzky and I left his office and went into the laboratory just outside it, where he introduced me to the graduate students who had helped him analyze the samples. Both were attractive young women, Dr. Mehdi a tall brunette wearing a sari and Mrs. Hartman, shorter and blonde, in a technician's white jacket. "Dr. Mehdi plated out the fungi, and Kathy helped with counts and slides. They'll show you what we found," said Stotzky. Then, glancing at his watch, he hastily excused himself and darted off, wearing the rather tense expression often found these days on the faces of the heads of university departments.

More than 300 petri dishes—shallow, circular, covered transparent containers—were piled on a long, stone-topped table, holding the fungi cultures from the four samples that had been investigated. I found the results bewildering—lovely, fluffy rosettes of pink, green, white, gray, black, and brown, sometimes mingled in a combination, sometimes merely monochromatic. They reminded me of certain surrealistic paintings of some thirty years ago, the coloristic abstractions that the Chilean painter Matta and the Spaniard Miró occasionally turned out. "We suspended ten grams of soil from each sample in ninety milliliters of distilled water, modified with rose bengal. Then we put one mil into each dish on a Martin agar medium," Dr. Mehdi said. From that, in three days, these astonishing flowers bloomed. On closer inspection the rosettes were filamentous, somewhat resembling cotton candy. They had recondite names like *Mucor, Fusarium,* and *Currularia.* One name that I recognized was *Penicillium,* a gray-green composition. It was a member of the same genus from which the antibiotic, now produced synthetically, was originally made. "The cultures look so beautiful," Dr. Mehdi said, "I almost haven't the heart to throw them out."

I next looked under the microscope at some slides of things that lived in the moisture of the soil. At magnification of 430-power I saw more bacteria, those prime workers in the vineyard of decomposition, which Mrs. Hartman said were a variegated bag—bacilli, *Arthro-*

bacters and *Agrobacteria*. At that relatively low magnification they looked like so many stars in the sky, some large and clear, some small and indistinct. The microscope's refracted light outlined their rather colorless forms with a pale, greenish hue. Another slide, with the microscope at 100-power, showed me an amoeba full of diatoms, which is a form of alga, and a protozoan with some bacteria inside it, both sights indicative of the jolly food fest that goes on constantly below.

Then Mrs. Hartman took some soil from Sample Two and placed it in a dish, into which she poured a little water, giving the contents rather the appearance of a small rice paddy. "The water may bring some of the macroanimals to the surface," she said. Sure enough, under the eye of the microscope, now at only ten-power, a nematode was visible, a small, thread-like object, wriggling mightily like an abnormally active eel. Its violent movements betokened a whole set of highly developed, if tiny, muscles. In the soil it sucks the juices of roots, its excrement adding to the earth's organic matter. Elsewhere, a white, eight-legged mite, looking like a diminutive mobile snowflake, scurried across the minute landscape, not in the least inconvenienced by the inundated surroundings, a creature that in the soil feeds on many things, including dead roots. Nearby, poking its nose out of the muck and rising to place its lobsterlike form firmly on a ledge of mica, was a pseudoscorpion, an out-and-out carnivore of the underground.

I next looked at Sample Three, the one from the meadow on Cedar Hill, which had not been analyzed. Under the microscope, still at ten-power, I saw that some of the root hairs of the grass had been replaced by interesting-looking, thick, knobby growths, the mycorhizae mentioned earlier, a symbiotic association apt to occur widely in trees and smaller things.

Secretions in general are also of primary importance in the soil environment. Almost all the creatures that live there are, naturally enough, sightless. Consequently, chemotaxis is vitally important. This is a phenomenon that only recently has begun to receive the scientific attention that it evidently deserves. It might be defined as the diffusion by living things of secretions that attract or repel other living things. It is a development that appears to be widespread in life. For example, in the human body the small phagocytes that fight infection are carried by the circulating blood until they reach the area infected whereupon they pass through the blood vessels' walls to attack the invading bacteria, being chemotactically directed toward them by secretions given off by the bacteria. Chemotaxis also may have been responsible for the dearth of bacteria that were found in Sample Four gathered from under the young maple tree in the Ramble, for tree roots and leaves, it is known, can secrete toxins. Whether this was the case or not, it is certainly true that chemotaxis is responsible for much of the movement to and away from living things in the soil by other living things. Virtually all of them emit secretions, and the moisture underground is ideal for transmitting them. Thus chemotaxis can be said to arbitrate and control much of the vast activity that goes on in the soil.

Following my departure from the biology lab at N. Y. U., I returned to Central Park, and walked over to the path on Pilgrim Hill where I had taken a sample. A rain and footsteps had filled in the hole that my trowel had made three days before. The ground now looked just like any other piece of trodden soil.

13

The Park's
Microscopic Water Life

Having discovered so great a microscopic populace in Central Park's soil, I naturally wondered whether a comparable number of things might exist below the level of our normal vision in the Park's bodies of water. As is the case with soil microorganisms, the species and numbers of their aquatic counterparts also depend acutely on the nature of the environment—whether they come from pure or foul water, warm or cool, shallow or deep, sunlit or shaded—and what I was looking for were the populations peculiarly native to the waters of the Park. These number a baker's dozen. Although in the strictest sense, all are man-made, for my purpose I divided them, somewhat arbitrarily, into two kinds—those I called natural, in the sense that they were designed to look like natural bodies of water in a natural landscape, and the others that are not in this class. The latter, sometimes utilitarian, sometimes recreational, are the reservoir; the sailboat pond, whose once-natural bottom has been concreted and is drained each fall; the Wollman skating rink, another part-time body of water but this one in the frozen state; the New Lake, formed on the site of the old reservoir; and the Lasker pool rink. The first bodies of water, those in my somewhat dogmatic natural class, are the Pond, where the ducks swim under the shadow of the Hotel Plaza; the Lake, with its rowboat concession near the Park's middle; and three sizable bodies of water near the northern end. These are the Pool in the northwest corner at the level of 101st Street; the Loch, a narrow rivulet that runs northeastward out of the Pool; and the Meer at the Park's northeast corner. Finally, there are three small bodies of water, all in the Ramble. This is a heavily wooded section that rises over the Lake, whose trees, often of foreign origin, were set out years ago to help make the Park a botanical showpiece. Two of these are Azalea Pond and the Swamp, a series of connected pondlets under the Ramble's trees. The third is the Gill, a stream that drains the Swamp and drops into the Lake.

From Dr. Stotzky I learned that his biology department had a knowledgeable man in the field of freshwater microscopic life named Dr. Henry I. Hirshfield, and I called Dr. Hirshfield at his office. Using Stotzky's name, I introduced myself and explained that I was calling because Stotzky and his team had found a dense population of microscopic things in the soil of Central

Park. I then inquired whether Dr. Hirshfield would be willing to test some of the Park waters for their contents along this line. He agreed quite readily, adding, "You know, I have long wondered myself just what there might be in the waters up there." By way of supplying a few details about the other experiment, I told him that in only the top three inches of a square foot of the Park's soil the number of bacteria, fungi, and other organisms counted had run into the billions. "Well," Dr. Hirshfield said, "it will be interesting to see just how many—and what—things are present in the Park waters. Life started in the water, you know. And a drop small enough to fit into the eye of a needle can reveal a bustling world of microorganisms."

The next day I set out to gather samples. Since I wished a fairly complete picture of what those Park waters that I called "natural" contained in the way of microscopic flora and fauna, I decided that a sample obtained from each end of the Park and one from the middle would accomplish this end. Accordingly, I chose the Pond at the southern extreme, the mid-park Lake, and the Loch in the northern area. I next bought, as Dr. Hirshfield had suggested, three screw-capped quart containers to hold the samples, a plastic shopping bag in which to carry them, a thermometer to take the temperature of the air and water, and a long-handled soup ladle to be used for dredging up a bit of the bottom, which is considered by scientists to be a part of the environment of freshwater microscopic things.

Thus programmed and equipped, I visited on a warm spring morning the three sites strung out over the length of the Park, reaching them by a combination of walking and riding in several taxis, a necessary method, since taxis could neither take me precisely to where I wanted to go nor park along the roadways of the Park to wait for a passenger embarked on no matter how momentous a journalistic errand. My thermometer told me that the air temperature that morning was seventy-nine degrees; the water temperature in the Pond and the Loch was sixty-two degrees, and in the larger lake sixty degrees. At each spot, often under the curious gaze and sometimes the puzzled questioning of onlookers, I ladled a container about three-quarters full of water and material from the bottom. I worked in the shallows just off the shore in order to duplicate as nearly as possible the top-level habitat of the flora and fauna that had been procured for the previous trial. As I had done with the soil samples, I labeled the bottles with numbers rather than the names of the bodies of water from which the samples came. However, I knew that Number One was the Loch, Number Two the Lake, and Number Three the Pond. As the bottom material settled in the jars, the contents looked merely like a floor of leaves-cum-mud covered by so much nearly clear water. Then I delivered the samples by taxi to Dr. Hirshfield in his office in a building off Washington Square.

While there, I inquired about the method to be used to determine what was in the jars. "We divide the tests for the jars' contents into those for plants and those for animals," Dr. Hirshfield explained. "This, of course, is simply for our own convenience. In the microcosmos, the actual dividing line between plants and animals is often hard to draw. The plants—by which we mean such things as diatoms, blue-green algae, desmids, and so on—are identified and counted by taking three portions of water from each of your samples in the amount of one milliliter, or one-thousandth of a liter, which is a metric measure just over a quart. A one-milliliter transparent slide with cover slip holds each portion. This is examined by a graduate student under a microscope at 200-power. Normally, this lets us see what we're after. However, we go to higher powers if, in the course of the examination, we come across some unknowns. Each round of observations is repeated three times by the student doing the tests, and I check the results.

"With animals," Dr. Hirshfield went on, "by which we mean such things as protozoa, nematodes, rotifers, and so forth, we first take an overview by stirring up everything in a sample and putting five milliliters of the turbid water into a transparent container under various magnifications. Twelve-power gives us the nematodes and the rotifers, fifty-power the larger protozoa, and one-hundred-power the smaller protozoa. Then, for further screening, we draw up one-twentieth of a milliliter in a pipette and place it under a cover slip, using magnification of up to 1,000-power. This provides us with what are present in the way of the smaller amoeba flagellates and the varieties of bacteria—coccus, spirillum, and rod. These last, of course, are generally considered to be plants, but for our own convenience we test for them with the animals. Finally, for the very small number of miscellaneous invertebrates apt to be found—such things, for example, as the tardigrate, which resembles a little bear—three portions of one milliliter each and a five-milliliter portion as well are examined under low magnification. This is because the objects sought are so relatively large. As with the plants, all observations in the hunt for animals and bacteria are repeated three times. Again, I check the results. The graduate students who will take the preliminary counts are Mrs. Sylvia Weaver for plants, Miss Janice Groth for protozoa and bacteria, and Mrs. Elaine Musnick for miscellaneous invertebrates."

Dr. Hirshfield said it would take a couple of weeks' work by him and his students to furnish a careful analysis of what the jars might hold, and I made a date to come back and see him when that was done.

On my return, Dr. Hirshfield asked me the same initial question as had Stotzky: Where had the samples come from? I told him the Pond, the Lake, and the Loch, giving him the numbers for each. "Well," Dr. Hirshfield said, "to summarize, the average count of organisms in the three bodies of water totals 7,500 per milliliter. This, of course, includes plants and animals, with the plants characteristically outnumbering the animals, in this case by a ratio of better than twenty to one."

I realized that the number per milliliter had to be cubed in order to find the total organisms present in a liter. Furthermore, in a quantity of water one foot square and three inches deep (the unit of earth involved in the previous experiment) there are slightly more than seven liters. Thus the average number of organisms present in the three bodies of water came to nearly 3 trillion, or a thousand times the present human population of the earth. Furthermore, if only the inhabitants of the most populous sample, that from the Loch, were considered, the figure rose to more than twice this, either quantity far outdistancing the total of 15 billion living things found in an equivalent volume of soil. I was astonished at the vast preponderance of water over soil life, and said so. "Well," said Dr. Hirshfield again, this time with a smile, "life started in the water."

He then went on to give some details of the analysis. "The main things we found were diatoms," he said. "Overall, in fact, they made up 76 percent of the population. Now, if you had taken the samples in cold weather, when the air temperature was in the twenties and the water close to freezing, the dominant organism would not have been diatoms but probably euglena, a green flagellate, sometimes called a plant and sometimes called an animal. Also such animals as rotifers and nematodes would have been down in numbers at that time. Diatoms, which we find in such quantity now in the waters, have a clear, boxlike shell of silica. They are photosynthetic. Scores of them could hide under a newspaper's period. They inhabit both fresh and salt water. In the spring and early summer they may cover vast areas of the ocean, just as they dominate the fresh water here. Also, they are one of the very most important staples at that very important level—the virtual bottom of the food chain, which is the network that administers all life. Tiny animals feed upon the diatoms, to be fed upon, in turn, by larger animals, and so on and on, the chain terminating in man."

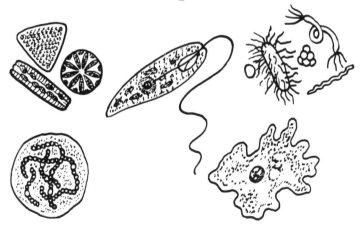

Microscopic Central Park water creatures. Upper left, diatoms; lower left, algae; center, paramecium; upper right, bacteria; lower right, amoeba.

Diatoms and other tiny plants in the food chain need phosphorus and sulphur to build their bodies. In the bottom ooze of all bodies of water live anerobic bacteria, including the ooze on the bottom of the Pond where the water descends to a depth of eight feet, the deepest spot in the Park's natural waters. The anerobic bacteria live in the absence of free oxygen, which the mucky ooze generally lacks. The bacteria feed on the dead matter entombed there, their metabolism releasing phosphorus and sulphur into the water, which the diatoms and other plants absorb. Thus in the Park the food chain begins.

I asked Dr. Hirshfield about the other kind of bacteria, the aerobic. They need free oxygen and can live interchangeably in the air, the water, or the soil. He said there had been some in all the samples that I gave him, although they were by no means as numerous as those in the soil experiment. In samples taken from a water body the levels of bacteria tend to be limited as sunlight has a germicidal effect on them. However, the coccus, a small round bacterium, was found in some quantity, as was also the spirillum, which resembles a corkscrew engaged in constant motion as it darts about, now forward, now back, while turning on its long axis at the same time. It is perhaps a surprising fact that one source for the aquatic bacteria is the actual soil of the Park. To design the natural waters there, the Park architects had to alter or cut off the flow of certain of the original water systems, both on and under the ground. To compensate for this, they laid pipes that would carry surface runoff from rain into the bodies of water. Accordingly, considerable quantities of soil bacteria reach them by these channels.

"Bacteria are the smallest plants known," said Dr.

Hirshfield, "and as such are at the very bottom of the food chain. On those in the water, therefore, rests the responsibility of maintaining not only the productivity of the water but its purity as well, productivity being inextricably tied to water purity. Maintenance of these twin objectives is, naturally, particularly important in the ocean, where so much of our food comes from. Both aerobic and anaerobic bacteria, as well as being used for food by animals further up the food chain, continually degrade dead plants and animals in their surroundings, releasing essential nutrients to be used by all organisms in the water for growth. This process of degradation keeps the water clean. Man has only recently begun to realize that he disturbs even this lowest link in the food chain at his peril. One way that he does so, of course, is by discharging industrial waste into coastal waters. Dr. Ralph Mitchell, Gordan McKay Professor of Applied Biology at Harvard, has pointed out that even if the waste does not kill living things, the level in some of the coastal waters is high enough to destroy bacterial chemotaxis. This is the sense—currently the object of much study—by which plants or animals are attracted to, or repelled by, emanations from other things, including foodstuffs. Mitchell has reported that bacteria in polluted waters remain mobile and apparently healthy but are unable to find their normal food even in the immediate vicinity. A pollution-induced barrier to chemotaxis thus threatens the foundation of the food chain. And today's broadening research shows other, often hitherto unguessed-at, threats. For example, PCB (polychlorinated biphenyls) is now a pollutant that is much talked about in scientific circles. It is a cousin to DDT and a thousand times as long-lived. Lately, it has been discovered in relatively high degree in oceanic plankton, some levels up

the ladder from bacteria but on which our larger marine life depends heavily for food. Since PCB is found
to be higher in the open ocean than in coastal waters,
the source must be the atmosphere rather than river
outflow. Thus an apparently innocent act by workmen
burning a piece of old painted wood (a PCB repository)
in a storage yard in Central Park would, through the
agency of offshore winds, add to the ocean's supply of
this pollutant, with consequent harm to the oceanic
food chain."

In the way of animals, a total number of thirty-
seven genera were found in the samples I gave to Dr.
Hirshfield, with, of course, some overlap among the
three sites. Fifteen genera were in the Loch, eight in
the Lake, and the largest number, eighteen, were in the
Pond. The genera comprised twelve photoflagellate
groups, twelve ciliate groups, six rotifer groups, an
amoeboflagellate, and six miscellaneous invertebrate
groups, including tardigrates and copepods, the latter
being crustaceans that love to feed on diatoms.

The Pond, which had the largest number of animal
genera as well as the largest actual number of animals,
also had the greatest quantity of blue-green algae. This
—a photosynthetic plant—was the second most numerous
organism found overall in the predominant plant category. The blue-green alga is one of the oldest forms of
life known. In the Transvaal in South Africa, far from
the waters of Central Park, stand the most ancient rock
beds yet found. They date back a full 3.3 billion years
to a time when the earth, now about 4½ billion
years of age, was barely 1 billion years old. Preserved
in one sequence of the rocks—a chert with a clear,
quartzlike quality—are microfossils. Also in the chert are
evidences of free oxygen, a substance that was virtually
nonexistent in the reducing atmosphere of the early

earth until the process of photosynthesis developed. Furthermore, the chert contained a far greater ratio of carbon-12 to carbon-13 than would be found in rocks that possess no remains of photosynthetic plants. Carbon-12, the lighter of the two common isotopes of carbon, is markedly preferred to carbon-13 by all photosynthetic plants for building tissue. The isotopes are then locked into whatever fossils may result. Dr. Elso Barghoorn, professor of paleobotany at Harvard, and his associates, examined these fossils, using advanced techniques of electron microscopy. They found these ancient things to resemble the single-celled, round forms of some of the organisms found among today's blue-green algae. In fact, they seemed quite similar to some present in my samples. "The two may, indeed, be virtually the same," Dr. Hirshfield said. "Blue-green algae is quite conservative genetically. It lacks a nucleus to carry its genetic material, a development that occurred after it appeared and greatly speeded diversity in evolution. When an organism has a nucleus and an advantageous mutation occurs, the new form tends to be perpetuated because the successful mutation's genetic material is duplicated in reproduction. A blue-green alga, on the other hand, has the genetic material scattered through the cell. It reproduces by fission— dividing in two. What produced the mutation almost certainly won't be duplicated in both daughter cells in the same fashion. This causes scientists to say that cells without nuclei tend to suppress mutations, allowing the master pattern to go on indefinitely when produced in favorable surroundings. A blue-green alga has been called an evolutionary relic."

I thanked Dr. Hirshfield for his analysis, and as I was leaving his office he handed me the three now-empty jars that had contained the samples.

Since I wished to get a look with my own eyes at some of the kinds of things that the samples had shown to be present in the Park, I telephoned to an old friend, Dr. Roman Vishniac, after I had left Dr. Hirshfield's office. Dr. Vishniac, who lives near the Park, has a broad capacity for friendship, which includes all microscopic water organisms. He is also a world-famous photographer of them, and someone especially good at showing them to laymen. I asked and got permission to bring to his apartment a sample of the Lake's waters for my personal observation.

Under his guidance I entered a fascinating world of the usually invisible. Through a microscope I watched bacteria, appearing as tiny, motile dots moving like stars across a silver heaven; ciliates swimming rapidly through the water, some resembling bells or wildly shaped women's hats, and rotifers turning round and round in a crazy fashion, as though bewitched. I also saw single cells of blue-green algae and other species of this life form, which were shaped like blue-green strings. "Ah, those ancient plants," said Dr. Vishniac. "Few living things are more secure than they. They are not on the verge of extinction. They are one of the most successful organisms in our midst." I then watched through the lens the watery passage of a diatom, a representative of the most numerous class of things in the samples given to Dr. Hirshfield and, actually, one of the most numerous organisms in the world. It was green because of its photosynthetic chloroplasts, and its little, pillboxlike case was beautifully striated. "Everything made by human hands is rough, ugly, and crude when enlarged," Dr. Vishniac said, "but in nature everything is lovely no matter how we increase the magnification."

Then he showed me a green paramecium, a protozoan, illuminated by a technique he called colorization. Under it, beams of polarized light break into colors when striking the crystals, which form living tissues at the molecular level. By it, internal organs and their functioning are brought out in vivid hues, which continually change as metabolism progresses. The paramecium, shaped like an oval sack, is turned into a many-tinctured jewel. At first, its nucleus was several shades of gold. Inside its body were violet plastids and blue and red dots and granules, moving on a pearly flood of material that circled inside the cell wall. "That pearly flood," Dr. Vishniac said as momentarily I surrendered the eyepiece to him, "is protoplasm, the stream of life." The colors changed and changed again. The tiny paramecium was a vision of awesome beauty.

When my viewing was finished, I took the sample whose inhabitants we had been watching back to the Lake. Dr. Vishniac makes this procedure a rule. He likes the organisms he has studied to be returned promptly to their place of origin once the study is finished. "To do otherwise," he says, "would be to disrupt family life. Just because some organisms are small, it does not follow that they have no rights."

As I dutifully replaced the contents of the jar in the Lake, I looked across its surface. Half a dozen rowboats, rented at sixty cents an hour from Riker's Restaurants, the concessionaire, were out there, their laughing and jesting passengers enjoying the afternoon sun. None of them, I felt reasonably sure, had the faintest idea of the teeming universe existing in the apparently empty waters over which they moved, or the importance of these watery inhabitants there and elsewhere in the world to them and to all others of us who stand, sometimes arrogantly, it seems, at the upper end of the food chain.

Index of Names

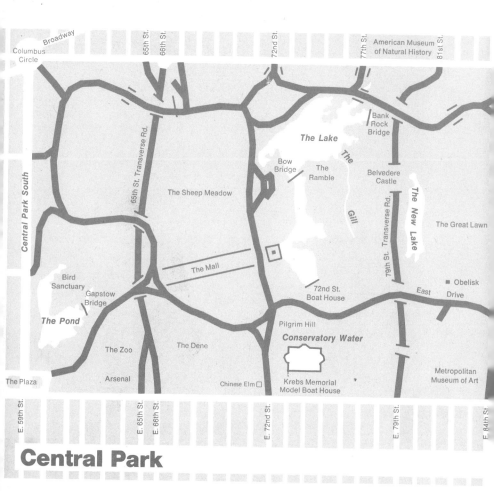

Central Park